ESCAPE TO PORTUGAL

A couple's Iberian journey

(Travelogue Series Book 3)

Author: David Gardner

ABOUT THE AUTHOR

David Gardner is a writer who spends his time travelling to beautiful parts of the world. He is a published author of books and scholarly articles and a bestselling author in travel writing.

David lives in Australia with his wife, children and a fluffball of a dog. His current passion is writing a series of travelogues from his journeys across the globe. He hopes you will share in his passion through these books and enjoy the journey.

ACKNOWLEDGEMENTS

My heart-felt gratitude to my wonderful wife, Wendy, who shares my trips, inspires me daily, infuses passion into everything we do and casts her critical eye over my work.

I would like to thank my colleagues for providing valuable feedback, and Ken, who has provided valuable proofing on this volume, giving generously of ideas for improvement.

CONTENTS

Why Portugal? I'm not sure how we arrived at this decision. The previous year Wendy and I had journeyed at length through the magic and romance of Italy in a wonderful cascade of emotions and experiences. We had also travelled to the UK in search of history and tradition. While traversing that island over several months, we'd trekked the Cotswold Way, a 102-mile adventure which provided many laughs, well developed leg muscles and memories that will never fade.

Portugal was selected almost randomly. We had toyed with the idea of Croatia, but had heard worrying stories about the swarms of tourists. We considered Spain; again, same issue. Destinations such as Japan, the USA and Czechoslovakia came and went. Then, after another few weeks and almost simultaneously, we both decided on Portugal. Neither of us knew anything about the country so we got to work. The more we read, the more we liked the idea until after some intense research, Portugal became our must go-to place. It had far fewer tourists than Croatia and Spain, in fact, was relatively undiscovered by travelling hordes. It was rumoured to be cheap, friendly and aesthetically beautiful, had millennia of diverse history, boasted eclectic architecture and of course, had the world-famous Port wine industry. Our question became, *Why not Portugal?*

Porto ... Arrival

Our body clocks were clearly faulty. After a 24-hour flight from Australia to Paris and a layover for several days in the romantic capital, we had adjusted too slowly to a new time-zone. Jet lag had hit us at regular intervals for the past three days, laying us flat out in bed at 3.pm and awaking us again at one in the morning. Now, emerging from a small plane that had been a flying party with two dozen intoxicated locals, we were exhausted. We were flying from Paris into the city of Porto in Portugal, and our middle-aged minds could no longer recall the time or in fact, the day that we inhabited.

I disembarked in dire need of a large glass of wine only to peer at the airport clock and with some shock, realise that local time was 10.am. Not a good start. The group of young Portuguese men who had disembarked with us are still in party mode. They are calling to one another, laughing and joking, buying each other more drinks, in no apparent hurry to leave the airport. Wendy and I on the other hand, are keen to find our driver for the one-way trip to Porto city. We also need to fill our lungs with fresh air, change into clean clothes and find something decent to eat. The driver from our apartment is standing outside the Custom's exit, holding a sign up with our names in almost indecipherable, tiny letters. He isn't much bigger.

Lucky to stand at five feet, he welcomes us with a big, sparsely toothed grin. Although small and thin and nudging what must be seventy years old, he grabs both our large bags, one in each wiry hand and strides off with all the energy of a twenty-year old towards the waiting car. It's all we can do to keep up. He can't speak English and we can't speak Portuguese so we trot along behind him in stunned silence. The three of us climb into an ancient Toyota which is thrust into gear and catapulted out of the carpark. The rest of the ride is just as hair-raising. Our driver hunches over the wheel filling the inside of the car with the smell of stale cigars and day-old liquor. He can barely see over the dash but his foot remains firmly planted on the accelerator, regardless of intersections or oncoming traffic. I turn to Wendy to make a face but her eyes are closed and head down. She's trying to remove herself as much as possible from what's happening.

In a very short time the car skids to a stop, our little driver turns and gives us another toothy grin and waves his hand, saying, "Out, out." Apparently, we've arrived. The owner of the apartment is there to meet us, handing the driver a few crumpled bills before he's back in the car and gone. She smiles and asks us to follow her before turning and striding off at the same pace as the ancient driver. The entire time, she's speaking in rapid, machine-gun fashion, telling us about the area and its attractions. Why are these people in such a hurry? We can't keep up with her physically or linguistically.

Wendy, as always, has worked her magic in choosing our accommodation. The apartment in which we're staying for the next week is divine. It's new, large, full of light, with floor to ceiling windows taking full advantage of the view. It's also in the best street in Porto, right on the Douro River but far enough from the tourist hub to remain quiet. This is the first time in Portugal for the both of us and it's a promising start. At first glance, the old city is small, bustling and entrancing. It is also full of colour. The tenements and apartments along the riverfront are bright hues of red, green, blue and yellow. They are primarily medieval, with many parts of the city dating back at least a thousand years, often further. Our apartment building is the brightest of the yellows, which is reassuring given our poor navigations skills. Further along the riverfront are several small restaurants, a little co-op supermarket and the usual tourist shops. It's time to unload, change clothes and explore our surroundings.

As we walk past restaurants, we're confronted with the most delicious array of cooking aromas, of meats, seafood and great vats of broth, all delivering pungent, earthy scents. Most restaurants have outside bars and table settings and seem to attract customers throughout the day. Menus on display tell us that whatever we decide to eat here will be cheap. And the further from the river you go, the cheaper the food. But it's difficult to venture far from this particular river with its wide, sweeping current, its swath of sparkling blue water, the small black Port boats that bob on its surface and the spectacular colours and lights reflecting across its surface. There is something about a beautiful river that captivates and enchants. It's difficult not to succumb to its spell.

The entire city of Porto appears to be built on a hill, with a steep walk to wherever you choose to go. This, we learn over our trip, is the case throughout Portugal. Many of the hills here are so steep in fact, that you find yourself bending into the slope as you climb. There is a myriad of tiny, winding alleys that lead you into a veritable warren from which it's mostly difficult to find your way out. They wind backwards and forwards across the hills leading you into even narrower laneways in which men sit talking and drinking their port wine or coffee while women hang washing, gossip in doorways or stand behind little tables, selling bottles of the unique Portuguese liqueur - Ginjinha. You can quickly overdose on these delicious cherry delicacies if not careful.

One of the pervading characteristics of Porto's enclaves, and really, wherever you walk in this city, is the music. Mostly, it's a form of traditional folk music (Fado) which emanates from small, private doorways, shops, cafes, bars, street musicians and clubs, and accompanies you no matter where you venture. It lends the city an air of nonchalance, but also frivolity. The Portuguese love their music. It is a constant at work or play and in a very short time, you are infected by their enthusiasm for it. We find ourselves listening for the different styles and genres and seeking out the cafes with the slower, more melodic Fado. But depending on your mood, you can always find a style and pace to suit.

There is an enchanting time warp as you walk these early medieval, narrow laneways, a glimpse into a way of life that for many here, continues largely unaltered day by day. These locals are fully involved with their daily rituals, just as their ancestors were before them, tending to their families and neighbours, engaged with the traditional intricacies of life, things that matter to them, but which most of us have forgotten. I suppose in many ways they represent the *real* Porto. It contrasts with the tourist drawcards along the riverfront, the celebrated restaurants, the hugely popular Port Houses across the bridge, the photo opportunities. But such tradition is certainly not confined to one or two ghettos. They are spread throughout the city, shining a light on a vibrant community reluctant to leave its traditional ways, a community that so far at least, is able to blend the old with the new without too obvious a strain. And it is this blending, in my mind, that adds to the lustre of Porto. There is vitality and energy as well as traditional charm.

Timeless legacies

There are, of course, mountains of history and tradition to blend in Porto. The actual city dates back to 300BC but the area has been continuously inhabited since the early Neolithic Age in 4000 BC. That's more than six millennia of civilisation. Porto has moved from scattered farming communities to Mediterranean outpost, the centre of feudal rivalry and global trading empire, with all the diversity and cultural richness that these eras have brought. Many of the families living here today are just the latest in a long line of multi-generational settlement, families that have lived in the same houses, working in the same crafts as their parents and grandparents before them as far back as they can remember. There are bridges, street planning, architectural marvels left by Romans, Goths, the Suevi and the Moors, and the small ethnic communities today still speak loudly of their own roots and journeys. Such diversity is far richer and more eclectic than either of us expected.

The Moorish flavour here is particularly pronounced. The Moors settled Porto between the 8th and 11th centuries and imbued the city with their distinctive architecture, culture, diet, farming methods and language. They even gave Porto its name, derived and shortened from Portugal to *Porto*. The peacefulness and relative prosperity of the Moorish period is possibly the reason why so much of their legacy remained intact. Unlike the Celtic,

Roman and Visigoth invaders, who attempted to subdue rather than coexist, the Moorish relationship with the peoples of the Iberian Peninsula was, at least after the initial conquering, more along the lines of 'harmonious assimilation'. They set about building roads, aqueducts, temples, palaces and city ports for trading. They shared the new-found wealth with their subjects, created rich agricultural farmlands, sustainable viticulture and enriched what had become a routinely pillaged settlement. In the long run such investment in the country and its people ensured a greater acceptance of Moorish values and practices.

It was not until the 14th century, however, that Porto realised its full potential. This was the ear of Portugal's maritime empire, an empire that emerged with the Age of Discovery and resulted in commercial dominance and a global reach of ocean-going trade. Specifically, the trade centred around Portugal's stranglehold on the very profitable spice industry and Porto became an indispensable base for its buying and selling. Complementing such trade was the development of the Douro Valley and its much-in-demand port wine industry. The Douro River emptied into the sea at Porto and provided the perfect transport route for the port boats bringing their cargo from the rich viticultural holdings along the valley to the world's markets.

Roaming Portuguese-style

For this week, we plan to take full advantage of all that Porto's history and culture, as well as its food and wine, have to offer. But first we need to acclimatise to these hills. Our apartment on the riverfront means that walking in all directions is going to be uphill. The Fado bars are uphill, as are the museums, the train station, the pedestrian streets, the supermarket, the parks and city tours. You name it, it's uphill. Still, I wouldn't swap it for the world.

For our first evening in Porto though, it's off to find a traditional fish restaurant and the one we settle on is just about next door to where we're staying. It's tiny, cramped, seems to have a fair number of locals and to be the real deal. What's more, it's advertising the traditional fish stew as its main dish! Wendy and I had read a lot about this national dish, as well as the warnings about avoiding the myriad of imitations that add extra ingredients and change the style of cooking. So before we sit down, Wendy, always seeking authenticity, checks with the chef on exactly how their stews are made. Apparently, it passes the test – fish (usually mackerel) prawns and mussels with potatoes, garlic and onion. No rice, and no other seafood. Down we sit, ordering a fish stew for two and a bottle of the local Douro wine. First, the obligatory free port is served. It's large, like a large glass of wine, except that the alcohol content is more like 20% than 12%. Wendy gives me a slightly worried look, I shrug and we start drinking. The meal soon arrives, spilling over its large serving plate. There is a pile of freshly cooked fish in the centre, surrounded by huge prawns and possibly two dozen mussels. We could smell the garlic as it left the kitchen and now, we're almost reeling with its pungency. The waiter is still exchanging pleasantries as both of us dive into the feast in front of us. It is one of the most amazing dishes I have eaten, rich, bursting with an array of delicious flavours, fresh and filling. It's also cheap. After half an hour of solid eating and washing the food down with our first *Douro* of the trip, we stagger out and look for somewhere to walk it off.

Wendy suggests a wander along the river-front promenade, where we can listen to the constant cascade of music from half a dozen bars along the shoreline. It is light, playful music, providing a perfect accompaniment as we enjoy the cool evening. Others are also enjoying the night, laughing, sitting in small groups talking about their day, or simply strolling as are we in the quiet of the riverside. Behind us, the city is alive. Music, car horns, lights, mass movement. Beside us, the great Douro River, broad and flowing in all its majesty, its surface like dark glass, reflecting the moving drama of a blood-red, setting sun. A little later, the surface comes to life as a flood of lights from the port houses, the great bridge and rows of medieval tenements spread out across its surface, stretching in luminescence from one bank to the other. An enchanting evening in an enchanting city. We find ourselves smiling in that subconscious, meditative way that comes with real contentment.

Early morning

The next morning plays out the same scene in reverse. Sitting at an early breakfast in our apartment looking out across the river, we watch as the sun climbs and sheds its silvery pink glow across the mirrored flow of water surging its way from valley to sea. The river is a lustrous crimson, and on each bank, sun reflects gold and turquoise and aqua as it strikes the brightly coloured terraces. Several of the traditional port keg boats (Rabelo boats) are making their way slowly, relentlessly upriver, laden with their valuable cargo. Others lie dormant, black silhouettes moored at intervals along its surface. Leaving our front door, we move in the early morning quiet before the city has woken, passing small gatherings of native residents, elderly men, retired, talking together in muted tones, already smoking their pungent cigars, enjoying the early solitude. This is their time. Wendy leads the way up onto the long, narrow bridge - the Dom Luis – which spans both banks, linking the residential with the industrial and commercial. Interestingly, the bridge, upon which construction began in 1881, was the project of Gustave Eiffel. And it's not too difficult to see the design similarities with Gustave's iconic tower in Paris. Amongst the warehouses and wholesalers sit the great Port Houses, awaiting their daily onslaught of visitors. Here are Graham's, Calem, Kopke, Taylors, Ramos Pinto, Offley Port House and Quinta do Novals. Today, like every other, their tills will open and the hordes will browse, taste, sigh in satisfaction and hand over their euros to purchase a small amount of the liquid gold for which Portugal is famous.

Houses such as Kopke date back to the 1600s; others such as Taylors and Graham's are fully or partially British owned and have been since the 1800s. Graham's the largest of all, dominates the

Port industry here, owning many of the vineyards and much of the land through the Douro Valley. This is where its world class grapes are grown and harvested, the vineyard workers living in tiny towns scattered through the Valley that dedicate themselves to serving the port wine industry. But more on this industry later.

By 8.am the city has come to life. Cafes are opening and already filling with customers, some visitors, but also many locals. The smell of strong, aromatic coffee wafts from their doorways. Several traders have set up in the square, hawking their wares, shops are rolling back their doors, entrances are being swept, the first of the day's washing is hung from upstairs balconies. Narrow streets are beginning to buzz with cars and people on their way to work, all jostling for position. In a very short time, the city is alive.

Rehabilitation Portuguese style

The locals we speak with through the week tell of Porto's changing character over the last decade. They explain that at last the city is taking pride in itself again, that there is new life and neighbourhoods are becoming more attractive than they have been for generations. More people are visiting, more people are staying. Americans, English, Australians, Scandinavians and Germans have begun placing Porto on their 'To Do' list. People are discovering that there is a fascinating side to Portugal outside the over-run and over-burdened Algarve in the south. And Porto, like many cities now throughout the country, has emerged from its days of economic despair and stagnation, witnessing a new wave of commercial and residential growth. The most obvious sign of this 'progress' *and* changing character is in the building works taking place across the city. On a single day I count thirty-seven cranes hovering over buildings in various stages of repair. Such activity reflects what the Portuguese call their *Rehabilitation Program.*

Although the Program was initiated in 1989 it has really only gained momentum in the past eight to ten years and has accelerated over the past five. The recent growth coincides with

Portugal's attempts, since the 2008 Financial Crisis, to extricate itself from debilitating debt. Under agreement with EU bureaucrats in Brussels, Portugal would roll back its debt and stimulate economic growth in an attempt to rectify a seriously ill GDP and current accounts. Unlike many of its European peers, the strategy is working. In fact, the country is seen as a template for restructuring a national economy and sustainable growth, and its citizens will relay these facts to you at every opportunity. They are rightly proud of what they have achieved. *Rehabilitation* is seen as an integral component of such sustained growth, and it's not only happening in Porto but in most of Portugal's major cities.

There are, however, strict guidelines about how this work is carried out. The Program is deliberately named *Rehabilitation* rather than *renovation* or *rebuilding* or *construction.* This is because of the ethos behind the initiative, one of bringing new life to what is already there, curing the ills but maintaining the history and traditions and the beautiful facades on these buildings. Rejuvenation of interiors, frames, amenities and accommodation does not dilute the integrity of the actual building. I wish they would come up with that idea in Australia. Anyway, the point is that it's certainly reinvigorating the city of Porto and giving plenty of people plenty of work while injecting millions of dollars into the local economy.

More fundamentally, it's also proved a catapult for the tourist industry. A significant number of the apartments and terraces undergoing regeneration are not just having new life breathed into them to satisfy local demands. Many are being improved to the standard expected by foreign visitors and tourists. These places will have a new identity as sparkly new Airbnbs or holiday accommodation. Portugal, and particularly places such as Porto, Lisbon and Coimbra, is at the beginning of a popularity wave. People are discovering a country of beauty, tradition, unspoilt landscapes and prices far below those of most European countries. Government, locals and businessmen have recognised and are now capitalising on the trend. Our apartment, for example, and the four others in the same building are owned by a small Portuguese company that rents every one of them out as Airbnbs. They are all brand new, beautifully equipped with high quality furnishings and are leased for short-term stays at a far higher return than your average long-term rental. It's all part of Airbnb's global rise. In addition, local business is also booming. Retailers selling everything from food and wine to clothes and mementos have never had it so good.

The economic upside to all this is obvious. But for locals, there is also a downside. For those who aren't participating in the Airbnb phenomenon or the retail surge, there are new pressures. As more and more apartments and terraces are bought by investors chasing these high returns, real estate prices in their beloved cities are rising quickly. This is forcing a number of the younger generation, whose families have often been living in these areas for generations, to move elsewhere. They simply can't afford the mortgages these prices require. And for the locals already living here, cost of living is also higher due to demands in all retail areas, from groceries and eating out, to transport, to appliances. The cost of living in the age of greater economic growth and a booming tourist industry is, for many, making life financially uncomfortable.

Lost in hospitality

The extreme gradient between the riverfront and the high points of Porto means that the streets and laneways wind their way backwards and forwards in circuitous routes to avoid the steepest inclines. Nothing is in a straight line, no grid pattern, no logical street plan. In addition, many of the lanes are only six or seven feet in width and criss-cross each other at an alarming rate. So, you might imagine that with Wendy's and my less than optimal navigation skills, this place presents a constant challenge.

We had been told by several people that the best restaurant in town was at the very top of the hill but since it didn't have a phone, we'd have to book in person. By mid-afternoon it's decided that we'll try our luck and set off in search of the place. After twenty minutes of climbing we are, of course, hopelessly lost. We can actually see the hill where the restaurant is meant to be located but for the life of us, cannot get there. No matter which road or lane we take we seem to end up roughly back where we started. On our fourth attempt we try a small lane that's much steeper than the rest, hoping it will cut through the melee of confusing choices.

After leaning into the hill and heading up the steep incline, I suggest a short breather about two-thirds of the way up. I look up and we're standing outside a narrow but tall terrace house of possibly three levels. In the doorway, two elderly men are sitting, one leaning against each door frame, playing some sort of card game. With broken English, one asks where we are heading and in non-existent Portuguese I explain with an assortment of single words and hand signals. A large smile creases his deeply lined face as he says, “Come, come,” standing and waving us inside. Wendy and I look at each other, not quite sure how to react. “Come,” he says again, waving us inside. So, somewhat hesitantly, we follow the tiny man inside. The interior of the terrace is dim and cramped and needs a coat of paint as badly as the outside. He leads us up a stone stairway to a small, spartan kitchen at the top. An equally elderly wife is sitting at an ancient table with a young woman, drinking coffee. The old man waves us to sit at the table, then produces three small tumblers and fills them with what looks like homemade Port. He says, “This will help,” and smiles again.

None of us can really converse in any meaningful way, so we simply sit and sip our potent Ports and smile appreciatively. He and his wife nod and smile in response. It’s the most unusual little gathering I think Wendy or I has ever attended and we’re not sure how long we should stay to show our appreciation, or how we actually go about leaving. I decide to drink my Port fairly quickly and Wendy follows suit, so that in about ten minutes we're finished and I'm trying to indicate politely that perhaps it's time to move on. Wendy stands and thanks them profusely for their kindness, smiling a great deal to make sure they understand. The old man follows us back down the stairs and the three of us wave our farewells. Yes, it was an awkward ten minutes of our day but the spontaneous hospitality that we were shown was very touching. It's something neither of us will forget.

Eventually the restaurant is found and a table booked. There is a queue of people waiting to do the same, which I think is a pretty good recommendation. At 7.pm Wendy and I are at a table for two in a small, crowded, authentically Portuguese restaurant. Waiters are rushing backwards and forwards between tables and the kitchen, as they try to cope with the volume of meals demanded. The dishes being placed on tables look monstrous but the people seem to be devouring them with little trouble. Service is quick, efficient and friendly, and a waiter is already approaching our table to take orders. I like the look of the meal that has just landed on the table next to ours so I point and ask for the same. Wendy orders grilled fish with prawns in a tomato-based sauce. For entrée, we order a selection of grilled and fried seafood and several sliced meats with seared potatoes. We have discovered that Portugal is a meat loving nation, and this restaurant is no exception. I also order a jug of house wine, which seems to be the standard among the customers around us. As our waiter leaves another comes with the customary glasses of free Port.

The meal is divine; a taste sensation of the freshest ingredients and cooked and plated in a no-nonsense style. There is no pretension, no theatrics, just really good quality food cooked to perfection. The helpings are huge, but our stomachs somehow fit it all in. Before leaving, I book a table again for the next night and then it's back down these steep hills to where, somewhere at the bottom, we hope to find our apartment.

The section of the city we pass through on our return is one of the oldest in Porto. Its lanes are more ancient, their cobbles small and uneven, and the width only enough to accommodate the medieval carts that once plied these parts. It's also the part of the city that is famous for its annual festival. The oldest and most traditional neighbourhoods here celebrate John the Baptist every year on the 23rd June and they have been doing so for the past six hundred years. But if you thought it was an event not to be missed, think again. You see, at each gathering, the locals (almost exclusively) and some invited friends, spend most of the night hitting each other with plastic hammers and garlic flowers. That's it. After they've extracted as much fun and excitement as they can, they go home. My obvious question is: How has this rather silly and mind-numbingly repetitive celebration lasted for six hundred years? Perhaps that's the secret.

Books, Blasphemy and Coffee

We awake to a dark, brooding sky with bilious black clouds hanging low over rooftops. The river is grey and sullen and swollen with discontent. The mood of the neighbourhood is sombre, visitors are few, locals stay indoors. But we have to find a laundromat to process week-old clothes which are beginning to take on a life of their own. Google tells us that there's one about three blocks from our apartment, at the beginning of the second incline.

For a reason I can't explain, we decide to leave umbrellas behind as we head out our front door, past taxi drivers huddled in their misty cars and begin our climb. Approximately half way and with no warning, there's an almighty crack of thunder, so loud that we both jump with fright. And then it starts, raining large, sloppy drops before, again with no warning, golf-sized hailstones pelt us from a green-black sky. It is the same distance back to the apartment as it is to the laundromat. We decide to stay the course, but these hailstones are relentlessly hitting home with real fury.

We're being targeted with rock-like balls of ice that are causing considerable pain. Disregarding pedestrian crossings, large dirty puddles, and the odd car we make a final dash for the shelter of the laundromat. I wrench the door open and Wendy, then I, splatter and squelch inside to come face-to-face with three other drenched tourists. The five of us stand in stunned silence for a moment, dripping into our own individual puddles before we simultaneously start chuckling. While checking for obvious injuries I reach up and feel blood trickling from a cut on my cheek. This was one vicious storm, but it's over as soon as it started. In a couple of minutes, the hail, then rain suddenly stops and the sun even breaks through a gap in the clouds.

Back in the apartment in a dry set of clothes we watch as the sky becomes a scattering of thin white clouds in an otherwise blue sky. Off again, and Wendy leads the way uphill into the centre of Porto, this time with umbrellas. It's time to explore the hub of the city. This is its essence, the epicentre, where tradition, culture and the daily hum of the city blend in a seamless infusion of activity. This area is not so popular with tourists, but it's where you can catch a glimpse of what makes this city tick, how its inhabitants interact and establish their place in the world.

First, it's up to Torre dos Clerigos, or what is known in English as the Tower of the Clerics. It's hard to miss. The Baroque Tower, built from granite, stretches some 75 metres or about 246 feet into the sky of central Porto, dominating the region and providing a clear navigational landmark for anyone at the top of town. The Tower is part of a church aligned with The House of the Brotherhood and was designed by Nicolau Nasoni in the 1750s. If you are feeling particularly energetic, you can climb (for a fee) the 240 steps to the top of the bell tower to indulge in a 360-degree view of the city and river below. On a clear day, the panoramic view is ample reward for your efforts. It is said that a particularly active Friar lived here and each day would climb the 240 steps to mount two white flags, announcing the docking of ships in the harbour below. In the years after his death it became increasingly difficult to recruit volunteers for this onerous task and the tradition was quietly forgotten.

From here, Wendy leads me across and slightly downhill to visit a famous and much visited bookshop. This is none other than the Livraria Lello Bookshop. From when it was first opened in September 1906, it has been a popular haunt of bookworms and tourists alike. It was owned by the Lello Brothers, who came up with the original idea of publishing and selling books more than twenty years earlier. With entrepreneurial urges getting the better of them, they turned their idea into a thriving business. This particular shop was the result of an eventually booming business that could no longer be contained within their original Chardron premises. The shop is of distinctively Gothic style and inside, is a veritable wonderland. After you pay your €4 just to get through the door, you are immediately confronted with a grand, beautiful, and mesmerising staircase that leads you in two opposing directions to the second floor. Halfway up, the staircase splits and divides into two semi-turrets that curve off to give you a full view of the shop and books on offer, before delivering you to the next, crowded floor.

As I said, it was famous and right from the beginning, demand tended to eclipse supply. But for the past twenty years the shop's popularity has become stratospheric. Hence their ability to charge you for simply entering the premises and, why you're more than willing to pay. This is all because of one little hiccup in recent history. When JK Rowling lived in Porto, she apparently gained much of her inspiration from the unique staircase and the Gothic atmosphere of the shop. So much so that she used it as the blueprint for the Hogwart's moving staircases in her bestselling Harry Potter series. When fans and non-fans alike learnt of this connection, they began flocking to the Livraria Lello and haven't stopped since. Now, when you arrive you are forced to line up for at least twenty minutes (up to an hour and a half in summer) just to get tickets. You then line up again to actually get into the shop. I think the selling of books has become quite peripheral, as the number of entry tickets sold each day ensures a constant river of gold right into the owners' bank accounts.

Similarly, the Majestic Café in Porto has become another major tourist attraction on the back of the JK Rowling connection. This connection does, however, seem somewhat more dubious. Urban legend has it that JK used to come to this café each morning to scribble her outlines for the book. The tale even goes so far as to suggest that she used to scribble them across the Café's numerous napkins, then collect them up and take them home for transcription. The big problem with this legend is that the Majestic Café is, and always has been, a very upmarket, sophisticated meeting point for the city's elite. They would visit for society morning teas, small, exclusive get-togethers served by aloof waiters in black bow-ties. Prices in the Café prevented the average Porto resident from frequenting other than for a special occasion. Given JK's income at the time was minimal and her means scarce, it's stretching a bit to suggest that this Café was her local. She was unknown in the town and certainly not one of the 'society set'. Nevertheless, that hasn't stopped the Café cashing in on the legend and the myths of JK's inspiration.

The real story behind JK Rowling's visits to the Lello bookshop and various cafes isn't nearly as glamorous as the outcome. You see, she actually lived for two years in Porto, where she taught English part-time, struggled with the language, and as a young, inexperienced traveller/writer, met a young Portuguese man. Popular legend has it that this enigmatic fellow came with a shady past, no regular job and a former drug habit. They met in a bar, he was fascinated with her looks and mind, they had a mutual love of books and in little time, were seeing each other regularly. Their relationship was passionate and intense, but also, at times volatile. Soon they moved into a tiny two-bedroom apartment together, but with little money, struggled to meet commitments. They married, Joanne fell pregnant, tragically miscarried but soon fell pregnant again.

Both were excited and looking forward to the birth, but according to the ex-husband, the relationship suffered with a new baby. Gradually, the volatility replaced the passion and the marriage broke down after one too many violent altercations. JK battled on as a single parent. Yet in that time, she *did* manage to continue her writing on the Harry Potter book and crafting what would become a masterpiece – the seven-book series. Locals claim she continued to spend considerable time in the Lello Bookshop browsing and obviously, memorising its visual splendour for future reference. The beautiful irony from her point of view, is that the man who had caused her so much misery severed ties with her and the child *before* her global Potter success and the substantial ballooning of her bank account.

Rowling's high-profile treatment at the hands of her husband and claims about his behaviour are at odds with the city's current push to curb all forms of violence and anti-social behaviour. For the past decade, city authorities, community groups and women's refuges have campaigned tirelessly and, to date, fairly successfully, to reduce domestic and other violent behaviour within the city. As in many communities, it was becoming a significant issue and a blight on the march towards a more civilised society. There is still domestic and other violence in Porto. But our volunteer city guide proudly tells us that the city is now considered one of the safer and more socially progressive cities in Europe. In fact, Portugal as a whole, claims to be the third most peaceful country, based on "safety, security, and politeness".

As campaigner efforts continue, they are even enlisting the help of their dominant religious institution – the Catholic Church - to fight this scourge. Portugal, like Italy, has a long history of embracing and being embraced by, the Catholic Church, and the country claims that almost 97% of the population still adheres to its religious teachings. "Mind you," our guide continues in a hushed tone, "a good number have let their faith slide and that you might consider only half this percentage to be actually practicing Catholics." Whatever their faith or otherwise, the Portuguese are using everything and calling on *everyone* to help in their pursuit of a safer community.

Faith and politics

The story of the Catholic Church in Portugal is similar to the Italian version. It has been the principal religion here since the country was ruled by the Roman Empire and is now responsible for twenty dioceses and approximately 2,800 priests. The official estimates reveal that the number of practising Catholics is considerably less than our guide's suggested 50%, currently standing at around one-fifth of the population. This, however, doesn't appear to have diluted the assumed authority with which the Church continues to speak. In fact, many of the country's elderly still recite the saying that, "To be Portuguese is to be Catholic". This belief is partly based on the extent to which religion has been encouraged by the Church and national leaders alike to infuse the cultural domains of the country's institutions. There was a formal separation between church and state in 1910, but informally, the links between the two are so interwoven that political initiatives are rarely taken without the Church's approval. Strengthening this legacy is the fact that for many years the country's health and education systems were within the Church's mandate so generations of Portuguese found themselves dependent on that institution's whims. I suspect it will take many more generations before such influence fades from daily life.

Political awareness generally, however, is on the rise. It is bewildering to hear from our guide that democracy only came to Portugal in 1974, on 25th April, in fact, after a rather relaxed, polite and peaceful revolution. It was a military coup, quickly overtaken by a popular movement of civil disobedience, as the population rose up to overthrow the country's authoritarian regime. It was so peaceful, in fact, that it was named the Carnation Revolution, a banner the Portuguese wear with pride.

Our guide relays what is for her, a very personal story of this revolution. She was a child of five and along with all other children, was sent home early from school that day, as it was believed that war could be imminent. She arrived home to find her parents huddled by the radio. When she entered, her mother rushed to her and swept her up, telling her that this was a great day for Portugal. Soon they would be a free people. She saw the excitement and relief in her parents' faces and began to cry. As she relays the story to us, there are again tears welling in her eyes. Wendy is also tearing up. But the passion of this woman for her country and its people resonates in a profound way.

Too much of a good thing

Wendy's pursuit this morning is neither religious nor political. As she has every day since arriving in Portugal, she's on a quest to find the ultimate Portuguese Tart, or *Pastel de nata*. These little delicacies are famous around the world for their creamy, egg custard fillings, lemon, cinnamon and generous wallops of sugar. And Wendy has become addicted. She has a list of vendors selling the treat and she selects a different one each morning to visit. Her quest, of course, means that before we do much of anything else each day, we must first find her day's supplier, where she will hover over the counter in tortuous indecision before selecting the latest indulgence. Her appetite is never sated, however, and her daily selection has grown in number from one to three so far. I fear this is an obsession that could quickly get out of hand.

By the fifth day, Wendy has become something of a connoisseur of these tarts and insists on giving me a full review of each one. I'm gluten intolerant so have little interest in such a national treasure, but that doesn't stop her. She compares and contrasts constantly. Fortunately, the fact that we walk everywhere and Porto's horizontally challenged streets, ensures she at least expends as many calories as she consumes. What I do join her in though, is the strong Portuguese coffee that usually accompanies these tarts. Together, the two treats represent a national past-time in Portugal. At cafés and bars across the city you will find small gatherings of young and old chatting over coffees and Pastel de natas. People will gather at any time of the day to indulge in these concoctions and why not? The tarts retail for approximately €1 each and the coffees at about €.60. It's a very cheap way of meeting with friends and sharing some company.

Interestingly, history tells us that Pastel de natas were born out of desperation. Created by Catholic monks in the late 1600s in Belem, the tarts were the result of frugality and dire financial conditions. The monks collected egg yolks as the primary ingredients in their newly created Pastel de natas. The tarts themselves were not the invention of idle hands, but rather, a frantic attempt to generate much needed funds after the wholesale closure of the country's monasteries. Due to a change of regime and an unsympathetic view of the role monks played in society, funding was cut off, and the costs of keeping monasteries open deemed unwarranted. The monks, therefore, suddenly needed to support themselves and fund new residences so they went into production, making and selling as many of these little tarts as they could manage. As with numerous artisanal products crafted by the religious orders, the tarts became a national, and eventually, global success story. Bakeries around the city and, in fact, the entire country, almost always have a line of people at the counter, waiting on their own selection of Pastel de natas. They sell as quickly as they can be made.

Similarly, Portuguese coffee has its own cultural identity that is adhered to almost as stringently as that of the tarts. Like the historical make-up of races along the Portuguese Iberian Peninsula, their coffee is a unique blend. Rather than using 100% Arabica beans as is fashionable in other coffee drinking nations, the Portuguese blend a slow roast of Arabica and Robusta beans, providing, what they claim, is a less acidic, stronger aroma with more body and depth. The coffee, referred to as "Bica" in most parts of the country, was named as such by the way it flows and falls from the expresso machine. It apparently simulates waterfalls or hot springs, which in Portuguese are referred to as Bicas.

To many Portuguese, this humble beverage has taken on almost Biblical connotations, as the population generally shuns internationally ubiquitous coffee chains such as Starbucks, Costa Coffee and McCafe, gravitating instead to the little artisanal producers of their own country. The rise of speciality coffees and coffee houses here has only added to the beverage's allure and perhaps also, its parochialism. After drinking my way around Porto, I think their coffee more than deserves its reputation. Wendy and I find ourselves craving this little heart-starter at all hours of the day.

Drunken journeys

Of course, our other newly discovered love here, is the amazingly popular Port wine. Having had it served up to us automatically and for free at every restaurant we've visited, this fortified liquor has worked its magic. Needless to say, Port originated in Portugal and under international copyright, can only be called Port *if* it comes specifically from Portugal. It also must be grown, harvested and made in a strictly prescribed manner. Grapevines have been cultivated in Portugal for the past six thousand years, making the country the oldest wine producer in the world. Port and Madeira, which are the fortified versions of Portuguese wine, have been favourites since around 2000 BC and have been exported to European devotees almost since the beginning.

The home of Port is the Douro Valley which nurses the great Douro River, extending from Porto to Pocinho, an area of 38,000 square miles or 98,400 square kilometres. It's an exquisitely beautiful region. On each side of the river, steep hills support vast swathes of vineyards that extend as far as the eye can see. The deep blue of fast flowing water contrasts with the even deeper green of the surrounding valley and the vibrant wildflowers that crest each hill. Throughout the valley are small, sometimes tiny, self-contained villages that support their own unique communities, steeped in a culture of the land and its soil. Serenity flows silently along this stretch of land, the river, the hillsides and the bluest sky providing a natural oasis for visitor and resident alike.

Today, we're indulging our new love of Port by visiting the great Port Houses that sit across the river, reminding us each evening of their silent, hulking presence with floodlit exteriors and brightly decorated signs. We set off at about 1.pm, walking along the riverside to the mighty Dom Luis Bridge, an historic icon of the city and one which spans 564 feet from bank to bank. Once, it was the longest bridge of its kind in the world, but that record, like the Portuguese empire itself, has been overtaken by others. From up here you have the most incredible views from the River's entrance to the sea at one end, to its disappearance into the deep Douro Valley at the other. And today, it rewards with sparkling waters below, blue skies above and the bright prismatic colours of the terraces that line each bank. It is what many would call a postcard setting and I'm sure there are many photos of exactly this scene.

Wendy and I stride along the pedestrian walkway beside four lanes of traffic, then down onto the opposite bank and head for the reputed best of the Port Houses. This is Graham's, and the whole place reeks of money. Graham's is the impressive legacy of two brothers – William and John – who created the wine company in 1820, through the payment of a debt that came in the form of 27 barrels of Douro's finest Port. The two English brothers were among the period's most successful businessmen, with extensive interests in the UK and India, and a relentless thirst to extend their empire. Little did they know just how successful their Portuguese business would become.

In 1882, another Scottish immigrant, Andrew Symington sailed to Porto at the tender age of nineteen to begin working for Graham's and by all accounts, exceeded all expectations. Not long after, his family saw just how lucrative the industry could become and moved wholesale into the Portuguese Port business. They built their empire quickly and successfully and soon extended their reach to absorb the famous Madeira Wines and Graham's itself. Today, they are the largest and most successful Port producer in the world. They own and control 27 estates throughout the Douro Valley and produce an astounding 70% of the Portuguese liquor.

This afternoon, Wendy and I are on a mission to help their thriving business as much as possible. We take our places in the Graham's tour, are shown the various aspects of Port making and a video on the Family's history. Then it is down to business in the tasting room. Lined up in front of us at our own table are vertical and horizontal tasting samples from some of the finest Ports available, accompanied by an array of cheeses that I think are intended to neutralise the effect of the liquor as much as anything else. Over the next couple of hours, as our host provides commentary, we work our way steadily through the line-up of large and surprisingly full Port glasses which, in hindsight, was a challenge we should have taken more slowly. The first few glasses delight our tastebuds with their different characteristics based on age, vintage and *terroir*. We have more difficulty distinguishing between the styles of the next few, the sixth glass I have trouble directing to my mouth, and after the ninth and final glass I can't get out of my chair. I look at Wendy who is leaning at a strange angle and having trouble putting her jacket on. Somehow, we find the exit and begin our journey back to the apartment. The thirty minutes it took to walk here turns into a two-hour meander back, through streets that I don't remember and a bridge that now seems to be swaying.

****

Nursing blistering headaches and attacked by startlingly bright sunshine on our final but one morning in Porto is not the cleverest or most pleasant way to start our day. We decide a gentle stroll along the river before turning uphill and into the city. Then we amble along to the Crystal Palace Gardens, which we figure might be the best way to neutralise remaining toxins from yesterday. It's another beautiful morning, and after some time the sun actually restores some life and vitality to our deadened bodies. The city is full today, too many people displaying far too much energy and sobriety in their pursuit of attractions. We stop at our favourite cafe for a strong dose of Portuguese caffeine before summoning the energy and will to view the Palace Gardens.

We're more than happy we made the effort. The Gardens look particularly vibrant today, blooming with colour and lush with an abundance of life. Visitors and locals alike are seduced by their tranquillity. But the gardens also tell their own Portuguese version of a great historical event in the quest of technological supremacy. You see the Crystal Gardens of Porto are the Mediterranean equivalent of the renowned and culture-shifting structure that made London so famous in 1851. The Crystal Palace was constructed in Hyde Park to not only house the Great Exhibition (or World Fair) of that year, but to squarely place London, and the UK at the centre of the world's fascination with 'progress and innovation'.

So, inspired by this remarkable achievement, the Portuguese decided to emulate, if not duplicate, the effort right here in Porto for their own series of exhibitions beginning in 1865. For the first year, there were almost four and half thousand exhibitors from across the Mediterranean and from around the globe, where they showed the world just how advanced they had become. Although a wonderful event in its own right, it never achieved the incredible heights to which the London event soared and remained forever a shadow of its predecessor.

Porto was never to attract the attention that was focussed on the fairs of cities such as London, Chicago, New York or Paris, but it *did* continue to hold its own exhibitions here and recently celebrated its 150th birthday. In 1952, the Portuguese Government, in all its collective wisdom, decided to demolish the Crystal Palace, casually expunging that decisive historical achievement from the City's memory, but the Gardens live on.

Today it is a sanctuary for exotic birds, threatened plant life and even hung-over visitors. It's an oasis of serenity from which you can look down on the city, the mighty River, and the medieval beauty that is modern-day Porto. The ghost of the Palace is still here. You can't help but think about that period of 19th century Portugal, as it lost its grip on an empire that had once been, lost the command of other nations vying for its trade, lost the capacity to compete in the new age of industrialisation. Perhaps the Portuguese removed the Palace for this very reason; they would no longer be reminded of what once was.

Enchantment and mystery

Our last 24-hours in Porto begins once again with breakfast in our apartment looking out over the river below. The moods of this river are so chameleon-like that you never tire of their displays. This morning the river is liquid silver with the sun reflecting sharply across its broad surface. More than ever, it's a symbol of strength and harnessed power. It transcends the full spectrum of emotion, becoming seductive, sensual in the soft, gentle colours of evening, shifting to an almost brooding, dark silence at night. With morning comes a radiant and dazzling display of confidence and then it relaxes into a grey, sullen meander as it supervises the city bustle through its daily routines. It's a fascinating parade of a river's majesty.

But under this spectacle are hidden profound depths of meaning. A potent, enigmatic river like the Douro, will carry with it millennia of histories and memories, narratives that have flowed through this land since the thawing of the last ice age around 15,000 BC. It will remember the first hunter-gatherers of the Iberian, the rudimentary long houses of the Neolithic farmers, the transition from nomadic to farm life, and from there, the unrelenting march of civilisation. It will record conquests, tribal wars, the mysterious symbolism of the Celts, the sweeping tide of the Romans and the totality of Moorish occupation. But this river has also shaped and remembered landscapes, brought much needed irrigation to settlements, transported food throughout the country, nourished each and every Portuguese civilisation, coursed the landscape in silence alongside hopes and pain, triumphs and despairs. In a way, it has been the essence of Portuguese history but also the messenger, carrying stories from one era to the next.

****

Tonight, we again witness Portugal's triumphs and despairs, through the sweetly melancholic music of Fado. This style is unique to Portugal, often described as the soul of Portuguese music. There is a following of devoted fans the length and breadth of the country, with each city claiming to be the music genre's home. Fado was born in the early 1800s, is known particularly for its sombre appeal, but has a myriad of variations to suit the mood of the day, time, or season. Newcomers to this genre are warned not to listen if already feeling disillusioned or bereft. In such moods, the music can only add to your misery. But it also has the capacity to take you places you would rarely visit, to beautiful places that leave you the better for being there. It is most commonly played in pubs and cafes and specialty bars, but sometimes also music halls of the larger cities, where crowds will fill the rooms to listen and participate.

Wendy and I enter a tiny hall in downtown Porto, where we take our seats among an audience of no more than twenty. The audience is dressed for the occasion, a few greet each other, known in the music circuit or perhaps just neighbours. There is an air of expectation, quiet excitement amongst us as we find our seats and settle in for what is, for Wendy and me at least, the complete unknown. Eventually, lights dim and a hush descends across the gathering. Two middle-aged gents and an elegant young woman of about thirty, walk onto stage and introduce themselves in Portuguese, then in English. With little more than a smile and a nod the two men begin strumming their tear-shaped guitars while the woman slowly immerses herself, and the audience, in the low, melodic notes of her first song. She leads us on a mysterious journey through heartbreak and sorrow and reflection before lifting the mood to one of inspiration and finally, passion. The audience is captivated. We feel compelled to follow her through a complex emotional landscape of poetic lyrics and exquisite melody. We listen to three songs in a row as the music flows through a full gamut of mood. It is all in Portuguese but somehow this doesn't matter. Wendy and I are swept up in the emotion of the singing, not needing words to appreciate what is unfolding around us. At the end of this set, guitarists swap, the style changes, but the singer remains. Four more sets lull us into an almost hypnotic state before abruptly, the woman announces that the evening has come to an end and thanks us for our time.

It has been an evening that neither of us will easily forget. We leave feeling blissfully numb to the noises and distractions around us, immune to the harshness of city life. We are soothed, almost catatonically relaxed. Our final day here is one we will remember for many years, one that has left an indelible imprint of serenity and an appreciation for the simple beauty that may touch you from time to time. It has been a remarkable gift, a memento to take with us on our next journey.

Douro Valley … Forgotten places

This morning we're travelling to Pinhão, three and a half hours down the train track from Porto. By car, it's only ninety minutes but as we are to discover, the difference is in the type and age of transport. It's only ten minutes-walk from our apartment to the train station, so we decide to lug our bags along the cobbled streets rather than wait for a taxi.

Porto train station, Sao Bento, is something to behold. Built on the site of an old Benedictine monastery in 1896, the station is a large symmetrically designed granite building that from the outside, looks more like an oversized courthouse than a docking platform for trains. Because of the granite it is cool, almost cold inside and crowded voices echo throughout the building's massive interior. But the *piste de resistance* of this station is the unique decoration within. Roughly 20,000 azulejo tiles in blue and gold cover every interior wall of the station, which are further surrounded by large azulejo paintings. Along the length of the great ceiling the tiles depict flowers of Portugal. These tiles were placed in the station over a ten-year period from 1905 and add a tangible beauty that few transport depots could rival.

Together, they reflect different scenes and eras of Portugal's long history. They also represent the themes of Portugal's progress, from pilgrim settlements through the country's farming development, the wine industry and the treasure trove that is the Douro Valley. Sao Bento is simply the most mesmerising train station you could ever have the pleasure of visiting. Fortunately, we mixed up our departure times and arrived 30 minutes early for the train, so we are able to wander at leisure and appreciate the full extent of this magnificent artwork. And what a superb idea, to turn an otherwise utilitarian passenger terminal into a stunning artwork that thousands of travellers will have the opportunity to view and appreciate and remember.

There's more to Sao Bento, however, than the stories behind these tiles. You see, the train station was built on the site of a 16th century Benedictine monastery – the Convent of São Bento da Avé Maria. Because of a decree issued in the early 19th century ordering the prohibition of all the Convent's male order and banning any new nuns entering the sacred site, it was left to the remaining five elderly nuns to carry on their good work. Under these conditions, the order was doomed to extinction, but these women were a sturdy old bunch. Despite the government's patience running thin and plans for development of the site, the last nun did not leave this earth or the Convent until 1892. Immediately, the government moved to tear down the Convent and replace it with Porto's newest train station. But according to popular legend, that final nun didn't give up so easily. While her body may have left, her spirit remained firmly entrenched, taking up residence at the new station shortly after it was completed. She is said to still haunt it today and if you listen carefully, you may hear her prayers and, I daresay, a few curses, echoing through the halls.

Too soon in our reverie, our own departure is announced and it's time to board. You could not expect a greater contrast between the glorious station and the train upon which we are departing. It is straight from the 1940s, complete with peeling paint, mismatched carriages and a diesel engine so worn that it engulfs the train and most of the platform with clouds of black smoke. This is one of the regional (Regionais) services and modernisation is still a fantasy. Inside, it's worse. Seats are broken, torn and dirty and the windows so smeared with grime that it's difficult to see out. Despite the dilapidated impression, however, our train pulls out of the station right on the dot, punctual to the minute and shudders its way into the journey.

****

The outer suburbs of Porto are much the same as in any large city, non-descript and scattered, with a messiness that belies their inhabitants' busy lives, varied interests, and often, financial hardship. Here though, we notice that virtually every backyard has been converted into a centre of food production. Relatively small spaces are filled to capacity with vegetable plots, small orchards and even smaller vineyards. Every square foot of space is utilised; no wastage, no prettiness, just much needed produce. Most yards have numerous chickens running free-range through the garden, no doubt supplying it with highly nutritious manure while keeping the family in much needed protein.

As our train journey continues, we pass through small towns and villages that duplicate this theme of necessary sustainability. The people are not simply following the latest fad or 'green initiative' by living off their small plots of land. Here, it is about subsistence living, reducing their cost of living to the bare minimum in order to *make ends meet*. Poverty is a common theme in Portugal and often most apparent in outer suburbs and satellite towns.

The average nominal Portuguese salary, for example, is just US$1,600 per month. In France, it's US$3,530, England, almost US$3,700, in the USA, just over US$5,000 and in Australia where I live, US$5,130 per month. Although Portugal's cost of living is also lower, its workers really don't bring home a lot of money, so you can understand why vegetables, fruit trees and grapevines are the dominant household plants. Houses in these towns are usually small, rather plain and often in need of repair and upkeep. They are what you might call *functional.* Money is spent on necessities only, with appearance a secondary consideration.

Progressing further along the Douro Valley, however, the landscape, both natural and man-made, gradually changes. Houses and villages are replaced by endless green colliding with the blue of the river. The terrain is dramatic. Steep hills cascade into the water's edge on each side, row after row of grapevines draw perfect parallel lines across hundreds of acres of hillside, with the first flower blooms just beginning to show. Villages are now rare and very small, perhaps hosting no more than a hundred residents. The small population out here may be found occupying substantial country houses on their own acreages. Large shade trees and ornamental ponds complement manicured lawns. The picture is more of gentility than subsistence. This is exclusive wine country and the affluence is hard to miss.

In another hour, our relic of a train pulls into the semi-deserted and rather ornate station of Pinhão, our destination for the coming week. There is nothing substantial about this town. When we first thought about staying in Pinhão, it was because I wanted to go somewhere off the beaten track, somewhere without tourists, without glamour. Well, let me tell you, Pinhão is all of these things and far smaller than I originally thought. The town is listed as having 600 residents but from what I can see, about 400 of them must be on holidays.

A simpler world

The steps down from the train don't nearly match the height of the platform so you must jump the last two feet while trying to haul your bag behind you. The station looks like a snapshot from the 1920s. Old but beautifully maintained station houses assume a substantial presence on each side, identical in size and architecture. They are a pale cream in colour, double brick construction, with deep eves of federation green that cast long shadows in the intense sunlight. Adorning the walls again are, the azulejo tiles that decorate Sao Bento station in Porto. Here, however, each is a masterpiece, standing alone and majestic. They are spaced at equal intervals along each wall, involving the most intricate designs and obviously maintained regularly. You can't help but feel the overt pride and respect that are shown to the most utilitarian of buildings. The station itself was built in the 1870s and opened for business in 1880. Its tiles were imported in the mid-1930s, a gift from the country's Port Wine institute and so, depict exclusively Portuguese agricultural practices.

From the platform you look up to the steep vine-covered hills of the Douro on one side, and the small, self-contained town of Pinhão on the other; one sublime, the other almost invisible. Other passengers alighting from the train appear to be locals. We are the only ones with bags and a traveller's aura. No more than one hundred feet along the platform, spread out under large overhanging trees are two families. I do a double-take, realising with amusement, that they are enjoying a picnic. I stroll down to take a closer look and see cooked chickens, various salads, soft-drink and the ubiquitous Port bottle sitting on a large, checked blanket. The picnickers seem quite oblivious to what's going on around them, in no way self-conscious of their incongruity. Wendy walks towards me with a broad smile, "What a wonderful scene, but why pick a station platform for a picnic?" she asks. Exactly my thoughts, but we're learning that Portugal is not quite fitting within our very Western ideas of 'normal'. The picnickers are happy and at ease. They're enjoying their relaxation, regardless or perhaps because of where they are. For us, it's what travelling is all about, experiencing such differences, appreciating diversity in the most unusual places.

To get to the town proper, you must first cross the train tracks. There's no pedestrian crossing or safety barrier, you simply jump down off the platform and cross in front of the stationary train, hoping that the driver doesn't get any homicidal ideas. From here, it's a five-minute stroll into 'town' along a footpath that varies in width between two feet and six inches and often disappears altogether. But it does take you past the most amazing array of retailers.

There is an auto repair garage with a 1970s fiat in about 2,000 pieces and the owner/mechanic sitting out front smoking a cheroot. He is half reclined on an ancient picnic chair with legs crossed, greeting passers-by in a most amiable manner. Not the usual image one might have of a mechanic. Next to his shop is, well, I'm not sure what it is. It's as if this owner has tried to cover the full spectrum of retailing in one shop. At first glance it looks like a butcher's shop, with slabs of cured meat on display and hams hanging from the ceiling, but there are also half a dozen bottles of wine on the shelf above the counter, several boxes of cereal *on* the counter, and stationary placed at intervals along one wall. Further along the street is a tiny, narrow doorway in which sits a woman who must be approaching ninety. She is in a dark, floral dress, has a book in one hand and what looks like a glass of port in the other. Behind her is a 'shop' that would be no more than three square metres. It has a grand total of four shelves. One has today's baked bread, two others have vegetables and the other is divided between cold meats and lollies. I don't see how you actually *enter* the shop because she and her chair effectively block the small doorway. Adjacent to her shop is a Farmacia (chemist) but no-one's buying today. Up ahead an ancient car is idling in the middle of the road while its driver chats with a couple of locals who lean on his door and look like they might have settled in for the afternoon.

Another 100 yards along the fickle footpath and a right turn at the stray dog lying stretched out on a blanket, we head up four steep flights of steps. Perched at the top sits our Airbnb in all its absent majesty. The villa, like the rest of the town, has been unsuccessful in extracting itself from the past. Outside, its walls are rendered in an orange/pink clay. Once we meet the hosts and are led inside, we see a small lounge area, a smaller kitchen and an even smaller bathroom. There are two dated bedrooms through an indistinct archway. A low-slung ceiling hovers precariously above as you make your way from one room to the next. The place could be best described as *minimalist*. A bare-bones villa in a bare-bones town. We knew before arriving, however, that the accommodation would be basic so there are no real complaints. The hosting couple are delightful and do their best to make us comfortable. Wendy turns a look on me that says, “So what are we meant to do here for the week?” I don’t really have an answer.

I start by checking out the view from the lounge-room window, which is quite breathtaking. We are surrounded by the steep hills of the valley and vineyards that stretch for as far as the eye can see. Down below, the little town nestles itself into shores of the river, quietly going about its business and looking like an advertisement for some out of date lifestyle programme. The cloudless blue of the sky completes a perfect picture. We forget about any drawbacks.

What’s called for this afternoon, is a walk and some fresh air as we’ve been sitting in a dusty, slow, uncomfortable train for far too long. Heading back down through the town to the river we turn left on the last street and pick our way along the bank for several miles. It is so quiet that the tiniest noise amplifies through the still air, insects, distant bird song, a fish plopping in the water below. We keep walking, enjoying the solitude, the panoramas of steep hills intersecting with the river, the vineyards, the endless stretch of river flowing through this vast valley, with an old boatshed or an ancient wooden bridge the only interruptions to natural beauty.

Many would see Pinhão as an escape from the world. It is very small, a frontier town almost, localised and traditional. The residents all know each other and have probably done so for generations. They have grown up together, work together, socialise, eat and argue together. The town has its own unique eco-system where outside influences rarely disturb the rhythm of life or the tranquillity that spreads out across this valley. Yet these people also welcome outsiders, are interested in them. They are happy for you to walk among them, participate for a brief time in their patterns of life. We are ready to settle in for the next few days and pretend all this is ours.

Cheap as chips

Feeling refreshed from the walk, we head back to shower and change for an early dinner, thinking we'll try the small restaurant we had spotted on an isolated stretch of bank across the river. On the way back through town, Wendy suggests we stock up with some supplies for tomorrow's breakfast and a cut lunch for our walks. We also want to sample some of these little shops that seem to treat normal retailing as an option-only past-time.

Wendy leads the way into the bakery first for some fresh bread. The loaves are enormous, and rustic, like they may have been baked in a stone oven during the Middle Ages. When she asks how much, the woman responds, 30c. We think we've misheard and ask again. Same answer. I think of the $5.00 or $6.00 per loaf we pay back home and wonder how on earth these people make enough money to survive. Next, we pop into a bottle shop and buy a "recommended" bottle of Douro wine for €3. Then, a packet of cereal €1, milk €.80c, a block of cheese for €.50c, and some ham for €.40c. So, for breakfast, lunch and a bottle of wine we pay the grand total of €6. We may have just landed ourselves in Europe's cheapest town.In terms of money, though, it may also be Europe's blackest. Pinhão's 'black economy' is thriving. No-one, and I mean no-one in this place, will accept credit cards of any sort. It is cash or nothing. I'm fairly certain a good percentage of that cash never finds its way into the accounting books. The first few times we ask about credit cards, the simple response is a lovely smile and a "oh, no *senhor*." I understand the cash incentive. Wherever you go in the world you'll find people and businesses who prefer cash, but here, it is a universal right.

A bit of simple research reveals that Portugal has one of the largest 'black economies' in Europe, approaching an astounding one-third of their GDP. This compares with an EU average of just over 16%. One analyst argues that in 2015, rather than the crippling deficit Portugal faced, if the 'black economy' was taken into account, there would have actually been a €4.1 billion surplus. We can safely assume that in its own little way, Pinhão, was a proud contributor to that statistic.

****

After showers and a change of clothes, it's back across the river to quieten our hunger pains in the small, lonely looking restaurant. The sun is setting across the Douro and casting long luminescent shades of crimson and mauve, with thin silver outlines. Tiny boats sit idle on the broad expanse of mirrored water and the banks are deserted except for two or three water birds dipping their beaks and calling softly to one another. The long day melts away, leaving in its wake a sense of calm, a quietness. We wander at leisure along the river bank, drinking in our surroundings, allowing the mood to wash over us, letting the evening sights and sounds and scents brush against our senses in their own time.

Entering the restaurant, we are shocked from our meditative state by the four staff who all turn and welcome us in loud unison. One stands at the large and primitive looking stove behind the counter. One is tidying chairs, and the other two sit at a small table engrossed in a game of cards. The two card players jump up and come to escort us to a table by the window, asking what language we would prefer them to speak.

"What's available?" I ask.

"We can speak Portuguese, French, Italian, Russian or English, whatever you like".
I give a small, embarrassed smile and reply, "Well, we can only do English."

"Perfect," he smiles, ushers us into our chairs and clicks his fingers, whereupon his friend glides from behind the counter carrying two over-sized glasses of Port. As always, the obligatory Port. We are the only couple in the restaurant, which is not surprising, given it's a Tuesday night. There are very few residents living around here, and no tourists. Both of us order grilled salmon and salad, which arrives soon after. They are two of the largest salmon fillets I've seen. The food is superb - perfectly cooked, fresh with a crisp, imaginative salad - all for €7 each. We feel guilty leaving, as if we should stay and somehow squeeze in another meal, just to put a reasonable amount of money into the till.

Wine, walking and sausages

I wake Wendy early and throw open the curtains to reveal another perfect day. The sky is a vast stretch of blue, the sun is glistening, the little town is already bustling and we are heading up into the hills for a long walk. Before we start, however, our host informs us that the walk up and along the ridge and back is around twenty-five miles, or forty kilometres, with some incredibly steep climbing. So, Wendy comes up with a better idea. We will catch a taxi up to the tiny village above, and take our walk from there.

But climbing into the back of the taxi I am quickly rethinking the virtue of this strategy. Our taxi driver is in his late sixties, I'd say, vastly overweight, sweating profusely, grey in the face, and really doesn't look long for this world. His continuous, explosive coughing only seems to confirm my opinion. He also appears to be having real trouble staying awake. After less than five minutes of driving, in which the speedometer never registers more than twenty miles an hour, I catch his almost closed eyes and stifled yawn in the revision mirror. And I can almost swear I just heard him snore. Wendy gives me a worried look and checks her seatbelt. But after another agonising ten minutes we are delivered safely to the little village above, Casal de Loivos, from where we'll take our first steps.

From this altitude, the view is astounding. Each direction, you look right along the Douro Valley extending for mile upon mile. Its great river, the lifeblood of Portugal, carves a broad, sweeping pathway through endless vineyards and beautifully moulded hillsides. Our tiny town is scattering of black spots far below, surrounded by the Graham family vineyards and their army of workers. It is silent up here. Eagles circle far overhead; the sound of the river is lost in the distance. This hill village of Casal de Loivos is eerily quiet, houses closed up, windows shutters snapped shut, no movement to be found. No signs of life. Even the corner shop is closed tightly, giving a clear message of no business today. We are reluctant to talk, for fear of breaking the silent spell. Instead, we sit for a while on a low stone wall overlooking the valley and a once in a lifetime view.

The day is warm but at this altitude the air is clear and cool, drying our sweat before we have a chance to heat up. Apparently, the temperature regularly climbs above 45 degrees here in summer, but today, it's less than half that. Walking at this height is invigorating, exhilarating even. Energy is flowing and we're striding out, putting several miles behind us before unexpectedly coming across a winery nestled down into the hillside. Unable to ignore such an obvious temptation, Wendy and I head down the narrow track to try the door. It opens and we feel obliged to enter. The winery is called D'Origem, and, according to the hostess who greets us, has been in operation since 2001. Before this, the site was the production centre of the family's olive oil business, where the extra virgin elixir was harvested, crushed and processed before going to market. The hostess is the owner's daughter, who is also now fully embedded in the business. She's bubbly, full of chatter and smiles, in a word, delightful. She leads us on an informal tour of the winery which includes the olive oil museum as well as the wine fermenters and bottling area, before settling us onto the balcony for some 'afternoon tea'.

Of course, there's no hint of tea in this little stop-off. Instead, we are brought a wonderful selection of local breads and cheeses to accompany far too many glasses of wine. The hostess insists that we do a vertical tasting of their classic vintages across several varieties and we don't want to dent her enthusiasm. There's nothing for it but to gratefully accept her offerings and dive in. Wendy and I sit overlooking this magnificent view, nibbling creamy local cheeses and sipping some really excellent wines for the next couple of hours. The sun sinks towards the horizon, the light becomes soft and our mood mellow. I wonder if there is any better way to live?

Eventually, with drowsiness threatening our return journey, we drag ourselves away from a hostess who wants the enjoyment to continue, and although I'm inclined to agree with her, my liver has different ideas. We make our unsteady way to the door and wonder how we'll negotiate the three miles back to Pinhão down a winding and unpredictably steep track. Sadly, there is no choice. There is not a single car to be seen up here, let alone taxi, and no sign of anyone to drive them if there were.

Roughly half way down the track, the first house we've seen on our descent looms high up on the left. It sits imposingly on a bank and as we pass below, two frighteningly large Rottweilers bound to the very small and ineffective fence, fiercely showing their displeasure at our presence. As they growl and bark and manage to show all their oversized teeth, I'm glad to see Wendy has learnt her lesson from England. Previously, she would have happily run up and shown her affection to any unknown dog. This time, she keeps her head down, making no eye contact at all. In fact, she's terrified, urging me on at a faster pace than I'm already managing. I'm happy to comply, however. These two aggressive animals look more than eager to leap the fence and show us what they're made of. Finally, the owner strolls out and tells them in a relaxed manner that perhaps they should behave. They ignore him and continue to leap up onto the shrinking fence, eager for a juicy morsel from our bare legs. I fear that if I look at them, they'll interpret it as a challenge and take up the offer all too enthusiastically. The slight headache that's been emerging from the afternoon's drinking session is now a full-blown, throbbing nightmare. By the time we make it past the house we're at a full trot, cursing the day Rottweilers were ever conceived.

After another hour of several wrong turns due to, by now, rather impaired navigational skills, our welcome little town pops up from behind a hill. Foolishly, I suggest we call into the 'butcher' to buy coffee from his random selection of goods. The fellow behind the counter is in the mood for conversation and plies us with questions about where we're from, why we're here, and our home country. He suggests that we sample his vast collection of home-made smoked sausages laid out in trays under the counter. We both decline but he's not having any of it. With great reluctance, Wendy and I become captive to his passion for every type of smoked sausage you can imagine. He places tray after tray in front of us and begins slicing for our tasting session. When his back is turned Wendy gives me a slightly horrified look and gestures that we need to make an exit. She's not much of a meat eater at the best of times and this selection in front of us is threatening to overwhelm.

He turns back and insists we try his samples so, slowly, Wendy and I work our way through a heavily seasoned, pungent range of not particularly pleasant sausage. By the ninth or tenth slice, Wendy's face has taken on a greyish hue and my stomach is begging for mercy. We hold our hands up and beg that he stop slicing. "Please, we can't eat any more." Still he pushes sausage towards us but we're becoming desperate, so push it back across the counter. Not perturbed, he smiles and says; "Now you must try my father's home-made Muscatel". We figure that it's at least a break from the meat so agree to a small glass each. He quickly disappears into the backroom and returns with a large smile and two equally large glasses of a bright orange liquid that somehow, just doesn't look right. We take a tentative sip as the fellow relays a long and sad story about this being his father's pride and joy; that he'll be so happy that we have shared his passion. Feeling a bit guilty, we drink some more, and a bit more. Eventually, we extricate ourselves from this overly enthusiastic retailer and make our way back to the apartment with an unwholesome blend of too much sausage and dubious liqueur washing around inside. We have felt a lot better.

Dinner with no name

It's 8.pm and hunger is pressing us to search for yet another restaurant. Restaurant visits are a must in Pinhão, as the store food selection is meagre indeed. There's no supermarket of any description, and food shops lining the one retail street offer a small, disparate and rather bizarre selection of foods that can't reasonably be put together in a meal. So, the search for new places to eat becomes a daily quest. This time it's found on the main street after a recommendation from one of the shopkeepers. Fronting up to the actual premises, however, is a confusing experience. There's no name on the windows, nor any sign of a menu. There is no indication of what the restaurant specialises in and peering through a window reveals a shadowy atmosphere inside with customers occupying several tables, but all waiting for their courses. There's not a glimpse of food to be had. Despite this, we go with the recommendation and push through the door.

Inside, all eyes turn towards us, as if we might be invading some private gathering. The manager peers out from the kitchen, stares at us for a bit, then returns to his preparation. We're not sure what to do. Perhaps this is some sort of club. Customers at the tables keep casting furtive glances our way, then turning back to their own discussions. Finally, the manager reappears and greets us with a simple "Yes?"

"Ah, we're here for dinner" I announce.

"Please sit", he says, and waves us to a table. He then turns and heads back to the kitchen with no more said. Continuing the theme from the window, there are no menus on the table either, or anywhere else in the restaurant for that matter. I'm about to suggest to Wendy that we find another restaurant when the fellow returns and with hands crossed in front of him, provides a rapid run-through of what we'll be eating.

"Tonight, you will be having four courses.

First is sausage (Wendy let's out a quiet groan).

Second, is white bean stew.

Third, you will have stewed pork and potatoes in white wine.

Finally, you will have beef cheeks."

Wendy informs him that I can't eat gluten. "No matter" he says, and walks off.

There is obviously no choice in what we can have and no indication of how much it will cost. Wendy starts to giggle at the situation but then begins to wonder aloud at exactly what we might be in for. Minutes drift by before the same fellow brings a single plate with a single sausage sitting in its centre. No vegetables, no condiments, nothing. He places it in front of Wendy, looks at me and says, "You can't have", and returns to the kitchen. Slightly bewildered, Wendy sits and looks at her sausage. Eventually, she tentatively cuts a slice from the end. "No, I just can't stomach any more sausage today" and leaves it where it is. My table setting stays empty. The next three courses are delivered in rapid succession, each large and each with several unidentifiable ingredients. The only vegetables in the four courses are the white beans, and a single potato. By the end of the final course, my trousers are uncomfortably tight and Wendy declares a day of fasting tomorrow. The bill arrives and as usual, it's ridiculously small.

Oh dear...

Yet another beautiful day dawns. The clearest of emerald skies promises more fine weather to come. But today, that's where the beauty begins and ends. We are thirty minutes into our morning walk along the river when our reverie is interrupted by an ominous gurgling from my stomach. I suggest that it might be prudent if we make a brisk return to the apartment. Once back inside, things go downhill rapidly. I suspect it is some sort of food poisoning, either the sampled sausages or last night's meal. Either way the bathroom becomes my constant companion for the rest of the day. What began as a day of so much potential is reduced to episodic misery and mortification.

Wendy stands by looking suitably sympathetic, but at a safe distance. She argues that there must be some other cause as she and I ate the same things and she's feeling fine. But as the sun sets, so does her wellbeing. For the next six hours we side step each other on our way to the bathroom and by midnight, I'm lying sprawled on the bed and Wendy's sitting on the bathroom floor. We remain in these parlous positions into the early hours of the morning, watching the light change with no enthusiasm for the new day. By dawn the trauma is finally over, but we're both exhausted, irritable and wanting only to assume horizontal positions for the foreseeable future.

This unfortunate event represents the closing scene on Pinhão and threatens to tarnish our impression of what is an untouched, traditional little town, nestled deep within a beautiful valley. Symbolising our sombre mood is a now steady rain that soaks us through on a cheerless walk to the station. We are bundled up in wet weather gear and umbrellas but somehow moisture continues to seep into our clothes, shoes and what feels like our very bones. And it looks relentlessly set in for the day. Lacking any vital energy, our sole mission is to board a train with the promise of better things to come.

Coimbra ... A Grand Old City

We can't help but notice that a number of people sitting in our carriage have their own Port wine bottles from which they are liberally filling plastic glasses. Port seems to be a permanent accompaniment to Portuguese life, regardless of where you are or what you are doing. In fact, relatively, the Portuguese consume more wine annually than those in any other country, amounting to a staggering 54 litres per head. This is more than France, Spain, Germany, Belgium or Australia, where half that amount is consumed. A large percentage of this wine is Port, followed by Madeira. Given that most Port wine is rated at approximately 20% alcohol/volume, you can safely assume that the number of intoxicated drinkers in Portugal at any one time is also higher than anywhere else in the world. But such intoxication only seems to make them happier and friendlier.

After three and a half hours on board this pre-war train, with tender heads and fragile stomachs, we finally pull into Coimbra. And the promise of better things has come to pass; the rain has cleared and the sun's shining again. Wendy and I haul our bags onto the platform, wave to our friendly and by now inebriated travelling companions, and head out to find a taxi rank. First, however, we divert into one of the local liquor shops to buy our own bottle of Port. Our fellow train travellers appeared to benefit from its soothing qualities and I have convinced myself that given the last 24 hours, it could well be medicinal. Besides, we have grown used to the delicious, potent, syrupy taste and figure we should join in this national habit of *drinking-on-the-go.*

We quickly locate and hop into a taxi, have a great deal of trouble explaining where our apartment is to be found, and then settle in for a hair-raising ride through backstreets, narrow lanes, blind corners and loud Fado music from our driver's cd player. In ten New York minutes, we're delivered to our waiting apartment, sitting on the crest of one of Coimbra's steepest hills. At least the view will be sensational. Our driver bundles us out and screeches off just as the apartment host materialises with a gracious welcome. He explains that our apartment is on the top floor. *They always are*. But he does offer to help with bags and chats energetically about the history and attractions of the town all the way up. Passing the first-floor unit, our host explains that the rest from here on up is ours. At the top of the stairs, we are welcomed into one of the most sumptuous apartments I have ever set foot in.

For what is a very reasonable city price, we are treated to a sparkling, freshly renovated apartment. It's in one of the city's historic buildings, boasts four large bedrooms, two exquisite bathrooms, a large lounge, kitchen, dining room, and private balcony overlooking the praca below and with views across to the famous University of Coimbra on the next hill. In addition, it is in the best part of town. My only thought is, "Wow!" and then realise I've said it aloud. Our host turns a proud smile towards us, and begins with the 'tour'. After generously presenting us with a bottle of good Portuguese wine, he bids farewell and we're left to admire our truly daunting accommodation. "I could stay here for a year," says Wendy.

For now, however, it's time to change and tour this city. We trundle down the stairs, out the front gate and into the winding laneway between old established terraces, to the city proper. The main street onto which we emerge is a hive of activity. Cars stream past and pedestrians dodge each other on the pavement as they wrestle shopping bags and children. Wendy's map tells us the next street across is a pedestrian-only street. So that's where we're headed. The European penchant for these pedestrian-only oases is a wonderful initiative. They allow you to escape the chaos of the city to wander at leisure along broad avenues and streets, paved with stone tiles or cobbles, lined by terraces and shops, cafes, restaurants, museums and relics from forgotten eras.

Coimbra has a number of pedestrian streets. The one we're on right now – Rua Visconde da Luz is in the heart of the city and a drawcard for visitors and locals alike. Its pavement is a mix of large rectangular paving stones and ancient cobblestones. On each side medieval terraces and shops and apartments crowd the sidewalks, keeping the street cool and immune to the traffic on parallel roads. Time slows down on these pedestrian streets. People sit at cafes chatting or stand in groups of three or four in the middle of the pavement, talking of their days and sharing gossip. You can wander at leisure backwards and forwards from one side to another, perusing shops, marvelling at the architecture or listening to ad-hoc choirs of university students who regularly come and entertain, raising funds for one cause or another. I have been here a little over two hours and already, I'm falling in love with this city, with its elegance and history and charm.

Beginnings

Coimbra began its life around the 4th century AD, originally under the name Aeminium, and then Conimbriga. Yet even today, there are rich deposits of ancient Roman archaeology, that mark the tumultuous birth of this first settlement. Like most of Europe, the city found itself at the mercy of several hungry empires, changing allegiances, religions, and fortunes over the next thousand years or so.

Control of Coimbra swapped between the Moors, who, for three centuries, exerted significant influence over architecture and prosperity, the Galatians whose idea of empire building was rather more short-sighted, and then the Christians with their cast of medieval kings. Throughout these disparate eras, however, the city generally survived intact. Its reputation throughout Portugal and much of the Iberian Peninsula was, for much of this time, one of well-being and enlightenment. In fact, the University of Coimbra, dating back to 1290, was one of the first in the world to be awarded university status. Today, its baroque library has over one million volumes, including a 15th century Hebrew manuscript that was hidden away by the University's librarians during the worst of the Portuguese Inquisition.

Portugal's first two Kings are also buried in Coimbra, which was the country's early capital for more than a century, 1151-1255. King Afonso the 1st ruled from 1139 to 1185, and King Sancho, who just happened to be Afonso's son, ruled from 1185 to 1211. He had one up on his father by also being born in the city. Wendy has planned to take me to the church where these two are buried sometime over the next couple of days, but this is another story. As with most Catholic cities, churches dominate here and are almost always perched on the highest points in the city, from where they assert their position and look down upon their flock. The Church claims these high hilltops were selected so that God's representatives could be as close as possible to heaven, but I suspect it may also have been to protect their original inhabitants from the dispossessed, often badly treated, and rather upset subjects.

****

As we stroll through this beautiful old city, the cold, clear air invigorates and clears our senses. There is an atmosphere of informality, of happy activity. People seem to be really enjoying themselves. Once again, we are reminded of Portugal's reputation for safety and peacefulness. There are no ugly scenes, no 'anti-social' behaviour, despite the numbers of people milling through the city. You could spend an entire afternoon just wandering these pedestrian-only streets, watching, listening, inhaling the marvellously rich scents of bakeries and restaurants delivering up their wares to an enthusiastic clientele. Almost subconsciously, we find ourselves blending with the city's vibe, taking on its energy and rhythm. Here, the unique melodies of Coimbra life surround us and right now, I can't think of a better place to be.

Many of the sights here represent distinct episodes in the city's history: the ancient, Romanesque cathedral, Sao Salvador, built in 1170; the equally old Monastry of Celas; the 13th century Convent of Santa Clara. The religious overtones of Coimbra's past, and present, are hard to ignore. But their architecture is sublime and lends the city a style, a certain status that allows it to stand out from its neighbours. And Coimbra does give the impression that it's a little different, a little special, a place where a more rarefied air sweeps through the streets, imbuing residents with a certain presence and civility. It has always been known as A Cidade dos Estudantes, or the The City of Students, and from the grand old University that sits atop Coimbra's highest hill, these students descend to the city below in their magnificent gowns, playing instruments, gathering in impromptu quartets, talking to locals, or simply strolling through their city with youth on their side and the promise of great things ahead. You have the strong impression that Coimbra *is* the University as much as the *Cathedrals*. Tomorrow's plan is to visit this University to see just what all the fuss is about.

Now, however, it's time to head back to our gorgeous kitchen with newly bought food to try our hand at some more Portuguese style cooking. Well, let me just clarify. I'm always relegated to the role of labourer, while Wendy whips up one excellent dish after another. She is quite a cook, and I really am *not*. Instead, I am forever chopping onions, garlic, chillies and other vegetables for each of her concoctions. I have never managed to progress beyond this point. Whenever I *have* cooked, I've managed to leave out one or more vital ingredients, actually *crucial* ingredients. So, it is now mutually understood that I will remain a 'helper'. I tend to sooth my battered ego with a glass or two of good red, while at my chopping station. But regardless of my diminished status in the kitchen, I do love the ambience of our evening ritual, preparing, sipping our latest version of liquid gold and listening to some quiet jazz. I wouldn't swap the time for anything.

Tonight, after unloading far too many supplies, Wendy has crafted a dish with all the flavour of Portugal. I've opened a second rather sumptuous bottle of Douro red and we have moved out to the balcony for *dinner with a view*. Wendy is in one of her philosophical moods; "This is what life should be. Travelling to wonderful places and just sitting back, appreciating their beauty." I can only agree. Too often, the modern variant of tourism demands that we rush through a country, see as many things as possible in the shortest time and tick off myriad imaginary boxes to boast about when we get home. Then we realise that we've simply *observed* from outside. We haven't actually *experienced* anything.

As a couple who like to travel, we agreed several years ago that we would adopt a *slow travel* method. We would take our time, travel through a region or country as thoroughly as possible, stay locally so that we could embed ourselves within the community, live where they live, shop where they shop, eat where they eat. Rather than pass through, you have the opportunity, if only for a little time, to *participate*. I think we have just about found the right formula. But that's just *our* method. Obviously, different things work for different people and different schedules. And, if you're really pushed for time, as enough people are to warrant the idea, you may spend a morning or afternoon at Portugal do Pequenitos, which means "Portugal of the Little Ones". Located close to the centre of Coimbra, this miniaturised reproduction allows time-challenged tourists, or those easily bored, to view all the city's significant buildings, churches, architectural marvels and monuments from a giant's perspective in maybe an hour or two. If you're feeling particularly adventurous, you may take an extended tour of the display and see other miniature countries as well, including India, parts of Africa, East Timor, and Brazil. The choice and style of travel is yours.

Tonight, however, we are both content to sit on our balcony and gaze across to the stately University of Coimbra. Its walls floodlit, its early medieval buildings glow a soft yellow as it looks down from a commanding position across the town below; the beacon of

Coimbra, the “shining light on the hill”, a symbol of the city’s progress and prosperity. An hour, two hours, pass in this state and we’re reluctant to take our leave. Instead, I retrieve another bottle of red from the kitchen and we settle in to quietly meditate on the fortuitous circumstances that have led us to this most intriguing country.

Gowns and iron bars

In a not-so-early rise and nursing stubborn headaches, Wendy and I suffer silently through breakfast and showers before heading up to the citadel of fame. The Old City is fascinating; each street lined with historic buildings four, five, six hundred years old. But it is also a rabbit warren. Streets and laneways intersect at odd angles, climb and dip steeply, and generally give you a thorough workout whenever you leave the front door. They also make navigation even more difficult than it normally is for us. What should be a short walk to the University is anything but. We descend for a good half mile before a strenuous climb back up the other side of the valley. There are laneways that end suddenly and from which we have to double back to find a new route. There are others that take us into someone’s workshop or private dwelling. Of course, there is, as usual, the mandatory navigational failure, in which we become so hopelessly lost that help is sought from various locals. Finally, however, the imposing University frowns down on us from close above.

About two hundred thousand visitors flock to the University each year, and in our first up-close glimpse we can understand why. Arriving from this route, you enter a vast courtyard that is surrounded on three sides by stunning architecture spanning Gothic, Portuguese Manueline and early Renaissance eras. They now house academic offices and the administration, but once were part of the palace apartments that hosted members of Portugal's aristocracy. On the fourth side of the courtyard, there is the most breathtaking view out over the city below with the broad sweep of the Mondego River bordering its eastern flank and the shadowy hills, blue in distant haze. A 17th century clock tower rises pinnacle-like from a medieval courtyard. Its antique clock still rings out the hourly instructions for academic life within. History tells us that in the day, after this clock struck its evening chimes no first-year student could be caught on the city's streets without dire consequences. From our later tour below ground, we are left in little doubt about those consequences.

If touring the University, you will come across grand medieval libraries, museums, Botanic Gardens, faculties both traditional and modern, as well as a range of theatres. It is a city in itself and in its earliest days was seen as a city apart from Coimbra and the rest of Portugal, a true 'light on the hill' that led by proclamation if not always practice.

Touring through the grounds, Wendy leads us into several museums and classrooms before heading to the University's Johannine Library. This single building houses some of the rarest and most valuable manuscripts in Europe. Today, some 24,000 students (about one-third of Coimbra's total population) have access to the wealth of knowledge contained within these walls, but when the University first began its life it only accepted sons and daughters from Portugal's wealthiest and most well-connected families. For many generations, the Library has also housed its own special colony of bats. These are left in peace in the ceilings and made as comfortable as possible because in return, they provide the critical service of feeding on the vast swarms of insects that would otherwise feed on the Library's ancient manuscripts.

We follow a pathway from the Library to the lower entrance levels of the campus. It's a strange feeling indeed to walk along pathways that thousands of students have walked to and from class for more than 800 years. You can only dream of their individual and collective expectations, fears and hopes as their destinies ebbed and flowed with changing empires. As it turns out, there was quite a bit to fear. Off from the Library is a long, dark, stone tunnel that leads to a group of damp cells with thick stone walls, tiny, metal-grated windows set safely out of reach and thick iron doors. This, believe it or not, was the Academic Prison, where misbehaving students *and* staff were incarcerated to think over their crimes. The crimes ranged from stealing to adultery, through a spectrum of 'inappropriate behaviours' while on campus. It was not uncommon for students to have their professors as cell mates for periods of several days to several months. The prison operated for a fairly extensive period, from 1782 through to 1832, and with its own law court, dealt out justice swiftly and at times brutally.

Perhaps the most evocative aspect of the University is its wholly owned Quinta das Lagrimas, which the Camões poem describes as the centre of Coimbra's most tragic love story. In the 14th century a refined and romantic royal by the name of Dom Pedro fell in love with the Spanish beauty Inês de Castro. He became so infatuated with her that he made her his mistress but the King, Pedro's father, apparently didn't like the idea that this love interest was the Lady in Waiting of Pedro's new bride. The bride didn't think much of it either. Waiting until the beautiful mistress was taking her morning walk in the Palace gardens one day, the King ordered her execution, on the spot. Well, this barbaric act led to a rather rapid decline in Pedro's mental health and when he eventually became King on his father's death, he ordered that his mistress' body be exhumed and placed on a throne beside him. His poor subjects were forced to swear allegiance to her as their Queen and kiss her putrefying hand each time they entered Court. A sad tale indeed but throughout this poetic tragedy, the long-suffering wife seems to have been completely ignored.

Fast-forward to today in Coimbra, and the latest scandal of forbidden love is somewhat lacking in such poetic romance. You see, recently, twenty-one government officials have been rounded-up by police for their dubious use of government credit cards. It turns out that apart from using these cards to buy furniture, groceries and petrol, they each had a penchant for acquiring their own short-term mistresses. These naughty little cards would turn up in strip joints and brothels on a regular basis, where 'services' would be procured. The mistresses never seemed to last more than a single night, but despite this drawback, the officials' appetite for their company remained voracious over quite a lengthy period. Perhaps not as romantic but for the mistresses at least, a somewhat less fatal outcome than that suffered by Pedro's lover.

Bells and bickering

No matter what hour of the day you wander through this intriguing city, you are accompanied by the ceaseless tolling of church bells. There are more than twenty cathedrals and district churches in Coimbra and they like to celebrate everything. Bells toll to announce the time, opening and closing hours, mass, any and all events through the city, the priest visiting the bathroom, or just the fact that someone's feeling happy. It's a melodic harmony that you never escape, that you come to expect. It is the background serenade of Coimbra. If, for any reason, the bells stop, you begin to feel something is wrong, that the resulting silence is unnatural, perhaps you should be heading indoors to safety. So, Coimbra is as much about sound as sight and taste. It is a relentless barrage of all senses, but in a marvellously good way, in a way that invigorates and tells you, you are *alive*.

The city is also a delightful and unapologetic mixture of the medieval and the modern. Along each street elaborate Gothic buildings intersperse between 20th and 21st century office blocks, shopping malls and high-rise apartment blocks. Tiny delicatessens squeeze themselves into narrow alleys beside 500-year-old churches, or a medieval cathedral that frowns down upon Moorish archways and tacky postcard stands. There is a strange harmony in this incongruous mix that the Portuguese take in their stride. You may wander through these archways into the medieval quarter, where cobbled laneways meander at aberrant angles past early Renaissance houses, four-hundred-year-old mills, textile warehouses. They relieve any modern perceptions that may still linger in your subconscious. Two great church bells chime their deep, sombre notes above, a rickety food cart rattles across cobbles that were laid in the middle ages when the plague was at its height of devastation. A large group of students from the University sweeps past us in full academic gowns, talking excitedly and running hands carelessly along ancient Moorish walls and the past eight hundred years simply evaporate. Suddenly, effortlessly, you are back in Coimbra's most embryonic years, watching an early medieval society slowly heave itself out of the its smothering Dark Ages to establish a semblance of community for its people.

Adding modern comedy to history, Wendy and I emerge onto a main road with cars parked on either side and traffic flowing freely and are treated to a slapstick encounter between a policeman and a fellow who is attempting to park illegally. The motorist has seen the policeman but appears completely unperturbed by his presence. The Officer strolls up to the car and wags his finer at the driver, telling him he cannot park here. To our shock, the driver winds his window down and begins yelling at the Officer, waving him away. The Officer leans into the window and sternly tells the driver again that he must move. It just gets better. The driver swings his door open in an aggressive manner, hitting the Policeman's leg and knocking him backwards. He then jumps out and lets forth a tirade of expletives at the poor law enforcer. The Officer throws up his hands in frustration and walks off, mumbling to himself. Wendy and I stare at each other incredulously. This is a first!

Wendy is planning another sumptuous meal at our apartment tonight, so I duck into one of Coimbra's many liquor shops to purchase a nice accompaniment, as well as, I am reluctant to say, another bottle of Port. We had planned to sip small amounts from our original Port throughout the trip but after two days, the bottle is empty. We chastise ourselves and vow that the next one will last longer. It turns out to be an unfortunately repetitive ritual of ours. Back in our kitchen I take up my role as vegetable chopper while Wendy dons an apron, rolls her sleeves back and takes command. I turn on some music, pour a little wine, and we indulge in a favourite pastime, cooking together. After this, we will again sit out on our balcony, absorbing the silence and watching the myriad lights of the city below as that beautiful wave of physical tiredness washes over us. We love the simplicity of life here. It's one of the things we enjoy most about travelling, the discarding of a pedestrian lifestyle, the burdens and stresses of normal, harried existence and instead, being alone together, doing what we love, cooking together, eating together, being enchanted together in a new country or city or little village that is far removed from the life we usually inhabit.

Morning breaks into a stream of dazzling light that floods though our front window. A soft breeze accompanies it, gently brushing the curtains and cooling the room. During a breakfast of cereal, fruit and coffee on the balcony Wendy suggests that this is the morning to make our way to Portugal's first two entombed kings. The Igreja de Santa Cruz is one of Portugal's most important churches, simply for its two medieval deposits.

"We cannot leave Coimbra without seeing this part of history. I have been looking at Google Maps and I'm pretty sure I know where it is. It's about three miles or so from here, on the other side of town. We can find somewhere out there to have lunch as well."

By the time Wendy's filled me in on the Kings' places in history and their particular deeds, I'm pretty keen to see these memorials as well. We finish breakfast, change into our walking gear, grab day packs and are out the door by 9.am. From our apartment, it's back down our much travelled, steep, winding lane to the town proper, about two hundred yards. Wendy is focused on her map and gives directions to turn right, while pointing to the left. This is common with her directional dyslexia, so I ask her to point again in the direction we should take. She points to the left down the main pedestrian street.

Looming in front, is a large, very grand and rather ancient church surrounded by a crowd of tourists taking photos. It is *incredibly* impressive, so we also stop, pull out cameras and click alongside them. A number of people are moving inside, still clicking. Others are taking selfies next to the entrance. We decide to keep on to our destination, but I have a vague misgiving, that there is a little too much fuss being made over this *one* church, when there are so many of them in the city.

Finally, at the end of this long pedestrian way we are thrust into heavy traffic moving in both directions. Wendy points ahead along the busiest route and says we have to stay on this road for about a mile. It's not pleasant. Car fumes cloud the air and fill our nostrils. It's noisy, the footpath is narrow, with little distinction between it and the road, and there's little shade from a very warm sun. We step out, trying to cover this stretch as quickly as possible. Suddenly, on our right, as if plastered onto this uninspiring landscape, rises the most exquisitely preserved medieval aqueduct, announcing the entrance to the Arches Garden. Such a beautiful but disconcerting sight, as it's the last thing you would expect on this road. Behind it are equally impressive gardens that lead into the much larger Botanical Garden. We consult the map again and figure that we can get off the obnoxious road and cut through these tranquil gardens, thereby cutting half a mile off our route at the same time. The gardens are shaded and beautiful, full of colour, impeccably maintained, and provide a magical relief from the traffic. We take our time strolling through, following the numerous pathways, appreciating this wonderful oasis. It's an imaginative, peaceful place to be.

A little way from the gardens, as we emerge from their gates, is the quintessential symbol of Catholic dominance in this city, and in fact, Portugal. Standing proudly in several acres of perfectly manicured gardens, with large turning circles, gravel pathways and commanding a most regal presence, is the imposing physical manifestation of Coimbra's Catholic Diocese. You can't help but be impressed, which is obviously the intention. There is no humble poverty here, just conspicuous wealth and power on full display.

The Diocese in Coimbra has a long history, reaching back to 563 AD. It had its power briefly curtailed during the Islamic conquest between the 9th and 11th centuries, but with the Christian *reconquest*, fully resumed its commanding authority within the city. At last count, sixty-five Bishops have served in Coimbra since the Diocese' inception. It covers an area of 5,300 square kilometres and serves just on a half a million Catholics (the total population is only 562,000). Unless the little kingdom of Portugal is again reconquered, the legacy looks set to continue. Whether it maintains the same level of authority that it's enjoyed for the past thousand years is another matter. We take our leave and head off in search of kings.

Another mile or so and Wendy's pace slows, her head buried deep in Google Maps. "That's strange", she announces. I give an internal groan. "According to Google Maps the church should be right here, where we're standing". At the moment, we're standing on the side of the road with cars streaming past. The only construction here is a green metal rubbish bin.

"It has to be around here somewhere", she says, trying to sound optimistic. "Let's just keep walking for a bit". We walk backwards and forwards for a while before Google Maps changes its mind and leads us to the centre of a large, bare, noisy roundabout. Traffic surrounds us. Foolishly, I joke that "the church doesn't seem to be here either", to which I receive one of Wendy's specially crafted glares. I shut up.

She suggests that we have lunch while we work it out, so crossing the road, a small grassy knoll is found, where we plonk ourselves down and open our, by now, warm and unappetising sandwiches. "Oh look", Wendy calls. To our right, stands a church. It's a nondescript, 1970s brown-brick church, completely unadorned, uninviting, and certainly not a place where you might bury two kings. I mention this discrepancy to her, but she's so desperate to find the burial chambers that she is up and walking through its door before I can protest. After peering inside, seeing that the interior is as uninspiring as its exterior, she checks her map again and reluctantly agrees to the obvious. I make some facetious remark about being glad I walked three miles in the heat to see a bland, forty-year-old church and receive another icy stare.

Finally, unable to glean anything remotely hopeful from Google Maps, Wendy gives up and suggests we head back to the apartment. The three-mile return journey seems even longer, hotter and more unpleasant than our trip out here. By the time we reach the pedestrian section again just below our apartment, I find it difficult to laugh at what would be an otherwise humorous situation. Pointing back across the square to the original and resplendent church we passed at the beginning of our journey, the one that everyone was frantically photographing, the one just 200 yards from our apartment door, Wendy wonders if that could be *the* church. Heading across to the entrance she asks the ticket-collector "if this might be the church where Portugal's first two kings are buried?" The ticket-collector gives us both a measured look, as if we might be a little slow and says "But of course" as she points to the banner proclaiming as much above the door. Wendy smiles at me sheepishly, and suggests we take a look, while I give the blackest frown I can muster.

Tomorrow we leave Coimbra for another of Portugal's wonders. We will miss the constant vertiginous climbs, the motorists who test their wits against you, the almost symbiotic flow from medieval to 21st century architecture and the sublime views from our hilltop apartment. We will miss the supermarkets, with their giant displays of salted cod that sit front and centre, drenching the cavernous interiors with an overpowering, ageing fish smell, the rows and rows of cured sausage hanging above every counter. We will miss their specials on Douro wine, seeing prices reduced from 3.99 to .99 a bottle. Most of all, however, we'll miss the almost mystical undercurrent of Coimbra. A city that has not only survived numerous conquests and occupations, but thrived because of them, taken on their culture, their inventiveness, their infusion of ideas, while refining and polishing them. Finally, a city that its residents celebrate and delight in.

Tomar … Home of the Templars

It's up early and a short taxi ride to Coimbra train station. Today we head to the famously historic town of Tomar, (pronounced *Tom-ah*). This was the home of the Knights Templar or simply, the Templars. These feared knights were of a strict Catholic order, originally recognised in the early 1100s, and remaining a viable force for approximately two hundred years. Their rise to power was rapid and terrifying and as their fighting prowess became legendary, so did their wealth. As leaders of many crusades, they of course shared in the spoils of their conquered foes and eventually accumulated so much wealth that they became a dominant financial and political powerhouse of their time. The Pope used them as an extension of his diplomacy, or more accurately, the final resolution in any unresolved dispute. As their power grew, kings and queens also courted them for their financial acumen and their ability to suppress any threatening force. They enjoyed astounding military success, for many generations commanding unparalleled respect among friends and foes alike. Tomar became their base, in which they built great castles and military strongholds, and from which they directed their influence.

What isn't so well known about the Templars, however, is that apart from their renowned secrecy, of which a little too much has been made, modern finance began with them. Their lending practices and insistence that new members deposit with their order upon admittance, built the foundations for banking as we currently know it. Their 20,000 members ensured that the coffers were always full, especially when regular top-ups flowed from new conquests. What further fuelled their wealth was the stringent code of frugality that was practised by all members. The Templars did not believe in luxuries or privilege, taking an almost perverse delight in eschewing these in favour of harsh, minimalist living. Deliberate deprivation was a common theme. Such a lifestyle eventually put them out of favour with the Catholic Church and its Pope, whose early adherence to 'poverty' was increasingly at odds with the way they now saw their place in the world. The traditional church was not quite as good at shunning the luxuries that wealth brought them, indulging far too regularly for most of their followers' tastes.

This divergence of lifestyle and beliefs led to rivalry and criticism and the Pope's lieutenants grew apprehensive about the growing power of the Templars. The one-time allies began to fear the Templars and suspect their motives, with King Philip IV of France and Pope Clement V eventually conspiring to bring about the dissolution of their Order. The Templar's political power, therefore, was gradually but relentlessly undermined, and as was common practice with forces that challenged the orthodoxy of the Pope, their wealth confiscated for the benefit of the Church. But the Templars did not fade into history. Their legend and a myriad of conspiracy cults that adopted certain Templar characteristics and practices remain to this day, building on the legacy and nurturing the myths. Even now, some of the fringe followers still believe the Templar order protects the Holy Grail and bequest them money in their wills to help with the quest.

The train to Tomar will take about two to three hours, depending on the mood of the train driver and how many unscheduled stops we make, which in Portugal, is common. So far this morning, we have made two such stops to drop passengers near their homes and once more to pick up a passenger flagging us down. No surprise then, that schedules are somewhat relaxed and fluid. Our train trundles along in slow motion. No-one's in a hurry and passengers appear content to chat and sip from their plastic glasses of Port wine.

Our cabin smells strongly of diesel. This is one of the fleet's older trains. It has paint peeling, carriage numbers are faded, windows are smeared and difficult to see through and seats could be a whole lot cleaner. But passengers and train staff are a constant cheerful and friendly presence. Perhaps, even with its age and dirt, this type of travel is preferable to those clean, sterile trains we have all experienced, in which no-one speaks, or smiles, or acknowledges your existence in any way. Each is locked into their own small world, usually confined to a 7cm by 3cm screen that absorbs their attention and interest, and ensures complete insulation from reality.

The conductor approaches, smiles and tells us that we must disembark at the next stop to change for Tomar. We thank him and gather our cases. The train slowly groans and creeks into Lamarosa station. Wendy and I, the only ones to make this change, step off to begin what we're told will be a half hour wait for the connection to Tomar. There is nothing. We are standing on a very long, wide platform and there is not a sign of life, *anywhere*. No amenities, no other people, no houses within sight, nothing. Wendy gives me a slightly incredulous look; “Isn’t this station supposed to be a major connection?”

“I thought so,” I respond.

There is no notice board telling us the time of the next train, where it is from or where it’s heading. But strangely, because of this isolation, I find the lonely platform remarkably serene. There is an undisturbed, untroubled feel to the place. The sun is shining in a deep azure sky, the sounds of small birds and crickets carry on a gentle breeze, and the rest is a profound, composed silence. I stand on the end of the platform enjoying the warming sun on my face and emptying my mind of all thoughts. The spell is broken by Wendy announcing, for the third time today, that she needs the toilet. “Well good luck with that”, I respond. With no other option, she eventually succumbs, crosses the track and disappears behind some bushes. I continue walking from one end of the platform to the other, trying to regain my sense of solitude.

Forty-five minutes of wondering when or *if* a train will come and if it is going our way, is brought to an end when we see snake-like carriages crawling around a curve in the distance. By the time the pre-war train pulls into the platform, another ten minutes have passed, but miraculously, it's *our* train. Off we set again. Almost an hour later we pull into the large, quiet station of Tomar, the end of the line. For the first time since we have been in Portugal, we're on flat land. Beautifully, wondrously, Tomar seems entirely flat. The station is old but as distinguished as the rest of the town appears to be. The arched hallway is cavernous and echoes with the voices of one other couple, who are waiting to board their own train. Two, disinterested station officials sit behind a far desk, engrossed in something below my eye-level. Apart from these small intrusions, the quiet continues, as if we might have brought it along the track with us. There is a population of about 20,000 here, about 40,000 in the entire municipality, but with little hint of tourists or tourist-related reception, it seems that for our stay at least, the company will be all local.

Tomar nestles in one of Portugal's most fertile regions, with a prominent escarpment ascending gradually from the end of town. The other obvious characteristic is just how pretty the place is. The late Gothic architecture is aesthetically beautiful; the roads and lanes are brimming with historic buildings, ancient shops, small, and well-maintained terraces, and there is a pristine, fast flowing river, the Nabão, that winds its way gracefully through town. Above all though, it is the relative absence of tourists which lends an authenticity to the town. There is no show, no display, just people living simply in this pretty place.

You cannot divorce the history of Tomar from its Templar heritage, each embodying the soul of the other. It is in the very fabric of the town, in its buildings and laneways, its festivals, its people, churches and convents, the stunning aqueduct that transported water to the Convent of Christ during the 16th and 17th centuries. Five minute's-walk from the Convent is the church of Santa Maria dos Olivais, built by the Templars on orders of the Grand Master in the 14th century. To me, this is every bit as evocative as the Convent itself (more later), a church where the ghosts of the Templars still seem to roam. You can feel their presence as you sit among the pews. It is a history rich in memory and culture and diversity.

Under Tomar, lies the ancient city of Sellium, the result of Roman occupation in the late centuries BC, but human settlement here actually dates right back to the mid Palaeolithic period of some 30,000 years ago, quite some time before the Roman Empire stretched its tentacles. Like so many towns and cities in Portugal, the Roman occupation heralded the beginnings of a series of foreign occupations. Tomar was later conquered by the Visigoths, who renamed it Nabantia and then the Moors, who settled here between the 8th and 12th centuries and whom the Templars battled with often and finally, victoriously.

But the town also developed a reputation for its enlightened approach to the plights of humanity. In the late 15th century, Tomar opened its doors to thousands of Jews who were being driven from neighbouring Spain, giving them protection and hope for a new beginning. Such enlightenment brought its own tangible rewards as these refugees brought with them their high-level skills and knowledge, as well as their horded wealth, a combination that invigorated the town and led it along a path of far greater prosperity. That relative prosperity remains to this day, surpassing many of Portugal's more renowned cities.

What you don't notice until you have been here for a while, is that Tomar's entire centre was designed as a cross, with a convent built at each of the four points. The design, of course, pays homage to the famous red cross worn by the Templars who resided in and protected Tomar for so long. The elegant red within white cross of the Templars not only dictates the city design, but can be found decorating bridges, hotels, public buildings, street signs, lampposts and almost any other surface that the residents can think of. It's a symbol that still resonates deeply in this region and echoes in each and every personal story.

Once again, because of Wendy's meticulous research, our apartment here in Tomar is not only charming, but moderately priced. It's located in one of the quietest quarters of the town, on a street that is obviously the focus of very proud landlords. There's a panoramic view to the end of the long, 12th century cobbled street before it climbs to the famous Convento de Cristo nestled into the foothills. A couple of elderly women sit in their doorway, as seems to be the custom here in Portugal, chatting with each other and watching for any unusual activity in their neighbourhood. There are possibly seven teeth between them, deeply wrinkled faces, wiry grey hair but ready smiles as you pass. They may have been sitting here for years; it looks like a daily ritual, a time in which they emerge from their domestic chores within to view the world outside their doors, and catch up on family and neighbour titbits. At the end of the street is a typical three-wheel Tuk Tuk, with a rickety cart attached to its rear. This is filled with an array of fresh vegetables pulled straight from the driver's garden with dirt intact, ready for sale around the neighbourhood. The terraces along our street are of white stucco with orange tiled roofs, all of the same style and colouring. They are usually two-stories, sometimes three and each has a large front door on the second floor leading onto a tiny, narrow balcony that only allows one person at a time. They are well maintained, regularly painted and clean. Each is the clone of the one next door and opposite. The feeling is one of an enclosed, intimate community, where proximity would encourage familiarity and dependence.

A block along from our apartment is the magnificent Republic Square boasting chequer-board tiles across its base and highlighting the spiritual centre of the town, Igreja De Sao Joao Batista, a 15th century church that stands proudly overlooking its flock. The Square itself is enormous and each day, and long into the night, it plays host to the neighbourhood, locals of all ages gathering to sit and talk, or stroll in couples. Young mothers sit and eat lunch while their children chase one another or throw ball, the family dog joining in the fun. Old men sit and smoke together, nodding heads in grave agreement, gazing mournfully at passers-by. The Square seems very much the centre of this community and the community revolves around its one thousand years of spiritual preoccupation.

In the afternoon of our first full day here, Wendy and I find a small, busy supermarket one block over and head in to stock up for the week ahead. Twenty minutes later we have a trolley full of fresh vegetables, fruit, yogurt, some chicken, minced pork, various sauces and herbs, plus garlic, onions and chillies. But I then spot four aisles of local and national wines; that's four aisles dedicated solely to wine in a supermarket that has perhaps only nine short aisles in total. Wine, of course, is an essential ingredient of any meal and in my humble opinion deserves all the space it can muster, but this is almost half the supermarket devoted to liquor. Without the tourist inflation of cities such as Porto or Lisbon, wine here is even cheaper than normal. We select five decent wines from a number of Portugal's best regions for less than €20 in total.

Laden with overflowing shopping bags we wander back to the apartment to unload and prepare dinner.

God's fortress

We wake from a deep, undisturbed sleep and look out to dull, overcast day. It is perfect walking weather, which is just what we need today. Our plan is to hike up into the hills above Tomar to visit the Convento de Cristo that everyone insists we see. It isn't a particularly long climb, but it has the reputation for being steep and taxing.

And it is. First the laneway leading up to stairs is long and of a gradient that gently eases you into a rhythm of complacency. The stairs, however, quickly dispel any notion of an easy walk, forcing several stops to catch your breath while pretending to take in the sights. All the while, the Convent, or fortress as it originally was, looms above us in all its mighty grandeur. The Convent, now a UNESCO World Heritage listing, attracts its fair share of tourists. At the end of March, though, Wendy and I enjoy the spectacle and history alone. At its base you turn and have unobstructed views of the entire town below and its lands beyond. It's not difficult to see why it was originally constructed as a fortress in 1160. Not only would the Templars have distant views of their many enemies approaching but up here in this stone stronghold, there would be almost no chance of defeat.

The most arresting characteristic of the Convent is its remarkable condition. Preserved over its 900-year life, today the Convent remains a superb symbol of living history, a beautifully maintained glimpse into the past, allowing visitors to build their own vivid picture of what life may have been like. The walls, of thick granite, are erected in already steep hillsides, running the perimeter of the Castle/Fort/Convent and must be twenty-five feet high. At the front, there are sturdy gates of iron and wood, with great iron rods running diagonally from one corner to the other. The walls themselves are punctuated every thirty feet or so by vast turrets from which arrows, spears, or any other projectile may be launched at an enemy who by this stage would surely be wishing they had stayed home. Once inside the gate, you're surrounded by an immense gravel courtyard, decorated with manicured gardens, hedges and dozens of orange trees. Placed at intervals, are long seats constructed from stone and covered in stunning Portuguese tiles of blue and yellow with intricate patterns. You can't help but be impressed as you walk through this regal entrance to the Convent at the rear.

In 2000, the now 76-year-old film director and ex Monty Python celebrity – Terry Gilliam -began filming his epic Don Quixote at this Convent. Epic it certainly was, because in 2017, he was *still* filming. He blames bad weather and other delays for the slow progress, which is a bit baffling, as bad weather doesn't tend to last for almost 17 years. The drama continued when at the end of this lengthy period, the Portuguese public broadcaster claimed that Gilliam's film crew had been less than careful at the sight. It accused him of damaging some of the marble within the Convent as well as uprooting several trees and breaking roof tiles. Sounds like they were busy doing *something* up there, even if not filming.

But controversy is not new to the Convent. It was also inhabited by monks who, from the mid-14th century, went by the title of friar. These fellows were assigned small, austere cells in which to carry on with their cloistered lives with the minimum of comfort or luxuries. They took vows of poverty, chastity, and obedience, but they were also highly educated, and had mostly come from well-to-do families. As was often the case in medieval monasteries, these vows did, from time to time, become a little monotonous. There was a tendency to spice things up by encouraging colleagues to 'misbehave' and take advantage of their seclusion. Prayers were regularly missed due to excessive hangovers, meat and fish were indulged in more than the once-a-week prescription, and wagered boxing was a common pastime. Guests, both male and female, were also known to stay for regular sleepovers. In other words, the austerity was more theoretical than practised.

Today, though, this magnificent Convent is a picture of serenity, cloaked in its Manueline and Gothic architecture, towering above us, inviting visitors into its cavernous, beautifully decorated interior. Its tiled walls, mosaic flooring, intricately carved ceilings and vibrant paintings clearly illustrate a rich heritage of paradoxical living. The tension between a craving for opulence, together with oaths of deprivation, was one that plagued these tortured souls throughout their tenure. It is, though, the quintessential medieval castle. Grey stone, endless turrets, small doorways and glass-free windows, dark, uninviting cloisters in all their Gothic manifestations, and the deep chill that permeates every corner of every room. It is difficult to imagine the constant struggle to keep warm in such places, with vast interiors, fifty-foot high ceilings, tiled floors and small, open fire grates, only one for each room, a totally inadequate attempt at heating.

Suddenly, our peace and tranquillity are ruptured by screams from the next room. They don't seem to be screams of fear or shock, but rather those that might accompany extreme anger. Wendy and I look at each other, not sure what, if anything, we should do. I creep towards the door separating the two rooms and crane my head around the archway. Immediately, I'm confronted by the most comic of scenes. I quickly wave Wendy over and we both watch in amusement as a well-dressed, forty-something woman is pounding her beleaguered partner around the shoulders and back with a rather large bag. She's screaming abuse at him about something he has, or hasn't done while he offers no resistance, instead, attempting to protect himself. In mid-swing she spots us at the door and abruptly stops. He also turns to see what brought him such good fortune. Seeing us, he calls out in broken English, "Is OK, is OK. Is my fault." With that, they turn and walk out through the entrance, her still hissing threats at him as they retreat.

That seems a fair enough conclusion to our tour and perhaps fitting, given what has transpired here over the centuries. Wendy and I also take our leave, heading back down the steep track into the town below. Arriving back at our apartment, it's already late and we had decided to head into the town proper to visit one of the local restaurants for dinner. Quickly showering and changing, we're out the door for the ten-minute walk to our venue.

****

Delights under the pavement

Arriving at close to 7.pm, we're the first customers. Portuguese, like Italians and Spanish, eat late, and Wendy and I are often met with curious gazes from passers-by and wait staff alike as we satisfy our hunger at such an early (Australian) hour. Tonight's restaurant – Tosca Moderna – scores highly on TripAdviser. From all appearances, it seems authentic, rustic and has a large, eclectic wine list. Exactly our type of restaurant. It is set down off the pavement, built of stone and polished wood and is small inside, providing a cosy, intimate atmosphere.

The barman welcomes us before the owner, a young woman, comes over to meet us. Both are very friendly, insisting that we take a 'proper' table upstairs. Wendy and I would actually prefer to eat in the earthy downstairs area, where we can watch what goes on and be a part of the front-of-house atmosphere. "But it's much nicer upstairs" the owner encourages. "Maybe," I say, "But can we eat down here?"

"Of course, but it's much nicer upstairs".

We assure her that downstairs is fine and, in fact, preferable. She shrugs and returns to the kitchen before the polite barman steps in to take our drink orders. Wendy asks him what he recommends but he's reluctant to make suggestions, instead telling us that he'll provide a number of samples and we can decide which we like most. For the next little while he lines up complimentary glasses of wine, one after the other, smiling and nodding at us as we try each one. I'm starting to feel light-headed before we even order a bottle. Next, as always, comes the complimentary glass of Port.

Laid in front of each of us is an extensive menu, running across several pages in Portuguese, with interesting English interpretations following. If the meals taste as good as their descriptions then I'll be a happy man. I can't help noticing, though, some of the strange names attached to their dishes. There are accompaniments such as "flavoured butter", "gizzards in peanut butter" and "crunchy scrambled eggs". These are followed by meals such as "kid in the oven" and "bright tripe". I let the owner know that I need gluten free food and she suddenly becomes very serious. "Of course," she says. "You let us know what you would like and I'll personally make sure it is completely free of gluten. Please do not worry." She runs through several dishes and tells me how she can vary these to ensure they don't contain gluten. At last, someone in Portugal who understands gluten intolerance. We settle for some of the more orthodox dishes as well as accompanying tapas. When the meals arrive, they are some of the most delicious we have tried in Portugal. The helpings are generous, the tastes delight our senses and the ambiance so suited to our mood. The bill arrives and again, it could barely cover the cost of the ingredients. I have real trouble getting used to the effort people go to here, to make such a small amount of money. I leave a generous tip and we walk home happy and full. The end of another day in magical, inexpensive Tomar.

At around 2.am, we're woken from the deepest of slumbers by the sound of hysterical crying below our bedroom window. It sounds like a young woman, with another male and female voice attempting to comfort her. It's no use. She wails interminably and loudly and their whispered comforts fall on deaf ears. We lie and listen for half an hour, hoping they will all get tired of the drama and move on. They don't. Eventually I get up, lean out of our window above and see three local teenagers, two trying to console the other, who looks about fifteen. From what I can make out, it seems she has been 'dumped' by an inconsiderate boyfriend.

Now, teenagers *do* love drama, but at 2.am right under our window is pushing things a bit far. I lean further out the window and loudly ask if they could please stop! I'm sure they have little idea of what I actually say, but the tone is enough to convey my message. As one, they all apologise and run away. They're obviously a lot more obedient here than our breed at home.

Morning breaks clear and bright with a brisk, cool breeze. First up today, we're visiting the local food markets, mainly to see what all the fuss is about (we are continually told that we simply must visit them) but also to see if we can pick up anything special that isn't available at home. After that, we plan to head off on another walk to the historic aqueduct outside Tomar. Walking into town you cross the Old Bridge of Tomar which fords the beautiful Nabao River. This takes us into the other, newer section of Tomar, which is less attractive, has a lot of businesses, restaurants, cafes and light industry. But it is also where the markets are located.

You can't help but appreciate the Nabao as you cross it. It is fast flowing, crystal clear and winds its way in an almost sensuous manner through the centre of town. Along its banks sit open-air cafes and several restaurants, a large, picturesque park, and huge willows that run along the river bank, hanging low over the icy water and sending their great roots deep under water for refreshment. There are also giant fig trees interspersed through town, and along the river as they surround the medieval watermill that still churns daily, creating tiny rapids under its wooden structure. The bridges that cross at various points date from around AD 100 through to the 1500s and are still the main thoroughfares from one side of town to the other. We vow to visit one of the cafes tomorrow, sip on a couple of local beers and appreciate the good life.

The markets, however, are a different story. As you enter the large sheds next to each other with interconnecting doors, you are thrown into a noisy, messy, frantic chaos. There are food stalls in every direction, selling every type of food imaginable. There are stalls selling just liquor and others selling only fruit. There are vegetables, cured meats, offal, fish, all types of seafood, cheeses, and stalls specialising in meats the likes of which I have never seen before and don't want to think about too deeply. For one stall, you need a particularly strong stomach... which I don't have. The meat is a strange, luminescent pink, in soft rolls that wind their way along the counter and give off the most unwholesome stench. The owner stands behind the counter expectantly but very few people visit his little counter of horrors. I feel my stomach flip, turn on my heel, and make a rapid exit. Wendy is already outside, looking a pale shade of grey and shaking her head. "How could anyone consider eating that?" she asks. We visit the next shed, select some aged cheeses and a bottle of Carcavelos wine, think better of purchasing one of the small jars with pickled unknowns, and decide some fresh air is a pretty good idea.

Wandering back through the Old Town, you are surrounded by very distinctive Moorish architecture. Villas, terraces, churches, museums, libraries all adhere to this magnificent style which evolved through five centuries of Islamic occupation, primarily from North Africa. And even though Cynetes (a pre-Celtic tribe), Romans and Visigoths also conquered and settled this land, it is the Moorish style that prevails. It lends the town a unique and proud character, a distinctive covenant that stands alone and apart in architectural genres. But above all, it is the aesthetic beauty that captivates. You can't help but be in awe of the classic lines and mysterious, even sepulchral overtones. You never tire of it and if you have the time, you let it take you where it will, turning down narrow alleys into the town square, cobbled backstreets that haven't changed in a thousand years, or along the life-blood of the river.

Today we let it take us via the Santa Maria dos Olivais and I remember the legend that hovers over this Church. For centuries, there have been claims that there's a secret tunnel running between the Church and the Castle high up in the hills. This tunnel apparently conveyed Templar Knights and monks undetected to and from the Castle and the Church in times of warfare and crisis.

They used it periodically as an escape route when one or the other was being attacked, but in peaceful times it doubled as a route that allowed them to avoid mixing with the masses while they travelled.

There are many myths and rumours about exactly what happened in this tunnel, some of them less than palatable, but the most enduring is the rumour that even today, the tunnel houses the world's greatest known Templar treasures. According to legend, there is an untold wealth in jewels, gold coins and spoils from some of the Templars' greatest conquests. Perhaps that's how Portugal managed to reduce its debt so effectively after the 2008 Global Financial Crisis. I suspect, however, that any treasure would have been plundered many years ago, and if the tunnel ever *did* exist it now remains nothing more than a crumbling and hazardous passage.

Next in our path home, is the Chapel of Sao Gregorio, where you are confronted by the other prevailing characteristic of Portugal – the number of people in churches engaged in silent prayer. In this particular church, we encounter at least eight, mainly women, scattered throughout the rows of pews, heads bowed, eyes closed mumbling quietly to their God. A couple of the women lift their heads to check our presence before returning to their vigil. We feel somehow blasphemous, merely sight-seeing while these faithful people are engrossed in such serious worship. I tentatively extract my camera in order to take some photos of the exquisitely decorated stained-glass windows, some of the best I have seen. I line up, click, and of course the flash goes off in all its glory, lighting up the dark interior. A woman lifts her head sharply and stares daggers at me while I make a show of cursing my “silly camera”. I put its cover on and exaggeratedly push it back into its case. She returns to her prayers after another meaningful stare. Wendy has, by now, discreetly distanced herself from the scene of disturbance, materialising in a dark corner at the back of the church.

We figure it’s best to leave our tour right here and head to our original destination – the Aqueduct. The town limits of Tomar are left behind as we head into the foothills once again. It’s roughly a three-mile hike to the Aqueduct of Pegoes so we have packed water bottles and a light snack. For the initial stages the track follows the same route that leads to the Convent but soon diverts and begins its relentless ascent. After leaving the track and navigating an old back road for perhaps a half-mile, the Aqueduct’s spectacular outline comes into view. I have to say that this first glimpse, in the midst of a barren, scrubby landscape, takes your breath away. We are in the middle of nowhere, with no sign of civilisation but this vast beautifully engineered structure. Its immense proportions and striking lines create an architectural masterpiece. Its height, the long, sensuous curves disappearing into the distance, rows of perfectly symmetrical arches and wonderfully aesthetic stonework really are something to behold. Most of all, however, is the pristine condition, a preservation that has lasted centuries with little sign of decay and looks like it could be put back into commission without too much effort at all.

The Aqueduct was commissioned under the rule of King Dom Filipe I, and is now just under five hundred years in age. Originally, it was constructed to deliver a vital water supply to the Convent of Christ and drew its supplies from four different sources in order to achieve this. Yes, this was a fairly dark period in medieval history, where tenant farmers and serfs struggled to live, let alone obtain anything resembling fresh water. But the first priority was always the welfare of the Nobles, regardless of the struggles elsewhere. And so, huge sums of money, man hours and resources were dedicated to ensuring that the six kilometres of engineering marvel would deliver an uninterrupted supply of Portugal's freshest water to the Knights and their monks day in, day out.

Whatever the reason, however, it is a historic monument to be appreciated, simply for its engineering feat and its captivating beauty. Altogether, there are 58 arcs and 180 arches built into the 100-foot-high structure, a structure that extends over rough terrain, through valleys, over hills and around cliffs. It is quite astounding. From a distance the colour is of a tan/cream stone but close up there are distinct grey hues. In keeping with the relaxed Portuguese safety standards, there are no fences or barriers barring your way. You can approach the Aqueduct, climb the steps and walk a narrow footway at 100 feet in the air, along its entire length. This is no mean feat. The steps up from the base land you in one of the small, enclosed guard houses that are stationed periodically along the wall and from here you can begin your high wire act.

Wendy, who is terrified of heights, anchors herself firmly in the guard house while I set off amid her warnings and worries along the ridge. The vista from up here is spectacular, with views extending right along the marvel of the Aqueduct itself, as well as taking in the panorama of deep valleys, agricultural fields, grapevines and rolling green hills in the distance. But I have to say, after perhaps three hundred yards, my nerves start to jitter and Wendy's warnings become all too logical. There are no safety fences, no precautionary measures, nothing to stop your rapid descent and unpleasant landing should you take a wrong step. And that's not hard to do. The ridge along which you must walk is uneven, with mortar and rocks jutting up in some places while missing completely in others. And, with a walking width of only two feet I'm beginning to feel like a gymnast, without the training. Returning to a relieved wife, we devour our snacks safely in the guard shelter.

Reverie

Our last full day in Tomar dawns and there's not really much planned. Taking an early morning walk through the Old Town, we visit a couple of local artisan shops before heading back to do a load of laundry. Much of the afternoon is then spent reading and sipping a little wine in the comfort of our apartment.

By 5.pm, however, we need a change of scene and remember the intended visit to the café on the Nabao River. Taking the short walk into town and across the river, we find a little café sitting serenely on the banks, bathed in a soft, late afternoon sunlight. I order a couple of Super Bock beers and join Wendy at a small, round table outside, with views across the river to the Old Town and the Convento de Cristo frowning down from the foothills above. It's a magical view. In the foreground on the opposite bank of the river is an old chapel immaculately maintained, it's whitewashed walls contrasting sharply with its red tiled roof. There is a sharp, pointed turret atop the roof with a cross at the top. Several other buildings with the same colour scheme sit either side. You could be forgiven for thinking you'd been transported to a small Swiss town and expect to see snow soon falling. The river flows strongly and freely in the foreground, the sound of its powerful current and the second beer we are now draining lulls us into a relaxed, meditative state. We both have dreamy expressions, not talking much, just absorbing this scene and the lifestyle of this ancient, sleepy town.

By another beer we are happily seduced, neither of us wanting to leave this blissful state. So, we don't. Instead, a simple, café-style dinner is ordered and we stay to watch the sun slowly set, gently illuminating the Convent and surrounding hills in a crimson glaze. Shadows lengthen across the river, birds settle in for the night, the twittering now subdued. A quiet descends over the town. The river maintains its own timeless journey. It cares not for us or the people inhabiting this beautiful place, continuing as it has for thousands of years, flowing through the course of human history, bringing new life, disposing of old, blending one civilisation with the next. It's a wonderful way to spend our last evening.

Lisbon … Chaos by the Sea

Our train for Lisbon departs at 10.28 am and it's only a ten-minute walk to the station. It will be sad leaving this lovely place. We have enjoyed its Moorish flavours, its ancient laneways and architecture and the simplicity of its lifestyle. But most of all, we've been enchanted by the physical beauty of the town. The Templars certainly chose suitably for their own "Paradise on Earth".

The train journey to Lisbon is advertised as taking anywhere between 1hr 40 and 2 hours. I'll go with the two hours. Again, the trip takes us through lands filled with vineyards, fields of olive groves and in between, the small towns and villages filled with the ubiquitous backyard vegetable patches. We have both been consumed with our e-books over the last hour but now Wendy announces that she's taking a break from reading. "Oh, great", I think. That means I am too. Because Wendy's other little quirk is that when she's finished reading, she wants to talk and I don't get much choice in the matter. I often try to keep reading, even asking her to please just let me continue, to which she responds "Sorry, I promise I won't disturb you again," and then keeps talking. I look up, raise my eyebrows. "Oh sorry, sorry", she says and thirty seconds later, is talking again. Eventually, I give up. Her reading habits are inevitably *my* reading habits. Wendy will usually end the conversation by saying how much she loves the fact that we do everything together.

So now we're both talking, but after not too much longer we're nearing the outskirts of Lisbon. The outer suburbs present a run-down, depressing sight. This seems a common condition of major cities the world over, so that often, your first impressions are completely at odds with the experiences you later have there. Our train slows to a halt at a large, broad and crowded platform. Towing our bags behind us we head for the ticket box to ask where a bathroom might be located, as we can't spot one anywhere. Wendy usually does the talking in these situations as I have found that officials respond far more enthusiastically to an attractive woman than a middle-aged man. But not this time. Wendy steps forward with a big smile and asks in her friendliest manner if the gentleman could indicate where the toilets are located. He stares dismissively at her and shrugs. "Do you speak English," she asks. "Of course".

“Well since you work here you must know where the toilets are,” Wendy persists. He just gives her his most insolent stare and remains silent.

“I really need to visit the toilet,” she continues.

He looks over her shoulder and calls, “Next”.

At this point I want to step forward and hurl a few expletives his way but Wendy grabs my arm and leads me to safety. It seems another characteristic that’s common the world over. Rude civil servants who are obviously dissatisfied with their job, or their position on the ladder, direct their frustration at an unsuspecting public. I think it increases their sense of self-worth somehow. Wendy crosses to the next booth and asks the fellow there. He helpfully gives directions with a smile.

Stepping out into Lisbon sunshine, the only thing between the station and Lisbon Port is a crowded main road, where people and cars dodge each other in a random and rather scary game of ‘catch me if you can’. And what a port it is, busy but beautiful. It’s nicknamed the Pearl of the Iberian Peninsula and it’s not hard to see why. At one end, luxurious yachts bob at their tethered stations while at the other, cargo ships load at docks. In between is the vast expanse of glistening water that seems to cast the whole seafront with dignified artistry. Such a contrast from the calamitous city it looks across. A light ocean breeze cools the crowds that lunch around the harbourfront before launching themselves back into the chaos. It turns out that our apartment is a slender 500 yards from this idyllic scene, around the corner from the station and up a steep, narrow street. When I say 'steep' I mean almost vertical, taking all our strength and willpower to haul our bags up after us. Even cars and Tuk Tuks appear to be struggling, the former grinding into first gear and the latter belching out clouds of choking blue smoke. Lisbon, it seems, is like the rest of Portugal, a series of increasingly steep gradients that crush your spirit step by single step. Struggling our way to the top, with several rest stops, I turn and look back over the magnificent view below. Small boats carve silver trails across stunningly blue water. People stroll along the waterfront and open-air cafes fill with coffee aficionados and early lunch goers. A cloudless sky hovers above, extending to the horizon, expanding a world before us. It is the quintessential Mediterranean scene and we are here to enjoy.

At last reaching level ground, Wendy checks her email and tells me our apartment block should be the fourth one along this street. The owner has said she'll be waiting out the front to meet us. Arriving at the front door, however, there is a clear and present absence of anyone. I knock on the door and we wait, and wait. Nothing. I knock again. Nothing. Ok, she's most probably on her way. We find some shade under a large fig tree and sit to wipe the sweat and rest a while. Wendy checks her phone but there's no message. After fifteen minutes I walk over and knock again, somewhat more loudly. No response. We wait another twenty minutes, during which time Wendy has sent two more messages, letting the owner know that we're here. Eventually, the front door opens and the owner emerges with a bucket of dirty water. We walk across to her. She smiles and asks if we're the Australian tenants, to which Wendy replies that we are and we arrived forty minutes ago as arranged. "Oh, I was just doing some cleaning," with no other explanation or apology.

The woman invites us in to drop our bags but says she hasn't finished cleaning yet, asking if we could come back in another hour. This is not a great start. We follow her up the stairs, past other apartments, and through a gradually narrowing space, to the very top floor. Ours apparently, is the attic, which was never mentioned on the website or by the owner. Opening the door to our 'apartment' (probably more accurate to say 'space') the first thing that becomes obvious is that it's nothing like the photos. It's tiny, and what looked on the website like multiple rooms is actually one long, narrow space. They have obviously indulged in some very creative photography. There's a kitchen that only one person can squeeze into at a time, a lounge area that only just fits a two-seater and TV, a tiny, mould-ridden bathroom that may not have been cleaned for a year, and a bedroom that is so small you can only get into the bed from one side. We dump our bags, give her a less than impressed look and tell her we'll be back in an hour.

Leaving the apartment, we feel somewhat deflated. Wendy turns to me and states in a way that does not invite a response, that we'll be scrubbing the place from top to bottom before we sleep tonight. For now, we're back out on the streets of Lisbon with an hour to kill. But soon our mood is lifting. This place is like no other place we've visited in Portugal, or anywhere else for that matter. It is chaos. The streets are full of locals, visitors, cars, trams, Tuk Tuks, vendors, musicians, noise and energy. The city throbs with the electricity of life, reminding me of somewhat rudimentary New

York or London. The streets vibrate with a coarseness, a grittiness, unrefined by Manhattan or Mayfair glamour.

Lisbon is life in its raw state, where the basics of living, trade, essential daily interaction, leave no room for the finer things of life. I have never seen so many people involved in so many different activities in such a small space. There are street-side bars, cafes, restaurants, terraces cramped one on top of the other, endless shops and boutiques, all welcoming and dispatching humanity *en masse*. You feel that if you stop, you'll be washed over and drowned by relentless turbulence. This is a city with a permanent adrenaline rush. It reminds me of an escaping balloon darting explosively around the room with no control or direction. After an hour of absorbing more than we can possibly take in, we're exhausted. Time to head back to the apartment to make the next week as comfortable as possible.

Wendy insists that we spend a couple of hours scrubbing every surface, as well as all the cutlery, crockery, sink, fridge and oven. I'm not sure what the owner did up here before we arrived, but it didn't involve cleaning. Apart from the obvious shortcomings of the interior, the apartment *does* have one of the best views in Lisbon. Our bedroom, living space and kitchen all have windows looking directly out onto the harbour below and the bluest ocean beyond. It is stunning. Obviously, the owner relies on the view to keep tenants happy, rather than the adequacy of the apartment.

We are located in the Historic Quarter – the Alfama. It is by far the most interesting and attractive part of Lisbon, with entertainment, curiosity and history oozing from its every ancient crevice. Within the maze of laneways, you'll find Moorish terraces with rows of washing hanging between windows. You'll explore the old Arab district, churches dating from the 1600s and even a rather grand castle. There are flea markets, cathedrals, museums, Fado bars, pedestrian streets and pracas (squares). But most of all, there is the sweet vapour of authenticity curling through every alley, every café, every cobblestone. This is the real Lisbon, and staying here, you cannot help but be part of the rich culture that pulses through this quarter.

The Alfama spreads itself between the Tejo River on one side, and the São Jorge Castle at the top of the Quarter's highest hill. Once upon a time, under the rule of the Moors, the Alfama constituted the entirety of Lisbon, but as the centuries have rolled on, so has the city. Today, the Alfama, represents a small pocket of a very large and colourful city. In fact, Lisbon, or as the Portuguese call it – Lisboa – stretches for over 100 kms in administrative terms, with a population nudging three million people, or more than a quarter of Portugal's total population. It is also one of the oldest cities in Europe, originating in the Neolithic period, roughly 5000BC to 3000BC. It was initially invaded by the Celts in the first millennium BC who conquered and then settled in the fertile Tagus River region. They lived well off the bounty of the lush region while consolidating forces and expanding their territory. Later, as with most cities in Europe, Lisbon attracted the attention of Rome, becoming one of the Empire's many conquests between 200 and 100BC. The Alfama was the centre of Roman occupation in this area, as it was with the Celts and later the Moors. As such, it hosts many disparate ancient relics and rich ethnic legacies.

The Alfama, suffered long periods of social and economic decline during the Middle Ages, and again in the Victorian period. In the 1700 and 1800s, particularly, the Quarter was home to Lisbon's poor and disenfranchised. Fisherman, unsuccessful traders, itinerant workers and prostitutes populated this historic district, with much of the district falling into disrepair. It was an area frowned upon by the Catholic Church, who warned its followers away from the district's temptations. The 'Good and Proper' of Lisbon would never venture within the Alfama walls, except perhaps in the secrecy of night to partake of the services of its painted ladies.

This is the story of Lisbon's greatest irony. For many a generation the religious fathers of Lisbon preached salvation through servitude to the scriptures and local priests. Comparisons between those who embraced their Lord and confessed their sins, and those of the Alfama, were a constant theme of Sunday services. Alfama residents were considered by the city's clergy to be beyond redemption, beyond the forgiveness of the Lord. They were a blight on society. Yet the self-righteous would soon rue their comparisons. Lisbon was about to succumb to the massive earthquake of 1755. And it was this act of God, which incidentally, ruptured the city in the very middle of the Feasts of All Saints celebration, that brought death to more than 10,000 good Christians. While praying in their cathedrals and churches, their world was suddenly shaken and torn down. The devastation was virtually absolute, *except* in the Alfama, where the thick stone walls and buildings endured the shock intact. Lisbon was flattened while the Alfama rose virtually untouched from its ashes, perhaps their Lord's own judgement on those who judge.

Today, the Alfama is enjoying a true renaissance. Holiday accommodation, rents and real estate are escalating with the increasing popularity of Portuguese tourism. Business is flourishing, cafes and restaurants are full. Culturally, this renaissance is even more noticeable, with the district hosting an increasing cache of poets and novelists, musicians and artists. There is a constant array of festivals, musicals, Fado concerts and literary tours. The money that now flows into the sector has created a mini-renovation boom amongst the district's traditional and often sumptuous terraces that first saw construction between the 12th and 14th centuries.

****

Tonight, we're too tired to cook so decide to take an early meal at one of the Alfama's many cosy restaurants. I spot an enticing little place about fifty feet from our apartment. It's small, intimate, and importantly, well patronised. Wendy, never one to make a quick decision, decides to consult TripAdviser for a more thorough investigation. And so, begins one of our trivial arguments. I am already irritable with hunger and weariness and ask provocatively why she can't make and accept a simple decision. "If we see a place that looks nice, then why spend half an hour looking for something else?" She responds with one of her cold stares and justification that, "Why not see what diners actually think, rather than just taking a punt and hoping for the best?" A few mild expletives fly backwards and forwards and I sarcastically tell her to try and decide before everything shuts. Half an hour later, she's finally found one. By this time, I'm ravenous. We set off, her leading, me following in sulky silence. After about ten minutes of this little pantomime, I ask how far this wonderful restaurant might be, to which she nonchalantly throws over her shoulder, "My GPS says it's another two miles." I let fly a couple more expletives, to which Wendy's fingers respond with strange sign language. By now, the silence and distance between us is further deepening. It's going to be a rather long and awkward dinner.

Next morning, with our argument all but a distant memory and moods significantly brighter, we decide to make an early start exploring the city. In her breezy, carefree manner, the host had warned before she left that while the shower had continuous hot water (what we call *Instant*), it did tend to get 'tired'. Graciously, I let Wendy take first shower and listen to a regular litany of yelps and curses as the temperature swings manically from scalding to icy. Apparently, there isn't much in between. By the time I enter, the pressure is tending more towards *exhausted* than tired. It has positively over-extended itself and is delivering a pathetic dribble of lukewarm water. Still, our spirits aren't to be dampened. We have one big, exciting city to delve into.

First on the list is a Portuguese tart shop in the district that Wendy had read about, a couple of hundred metres from the apartment. On the way, she relays a short story about the origin of these tarts, with the catalyst being what she describes as an *excess of eggs*. Only half listening as I try to take in all that is going on around us, I just hear three odd words. "Did you say an excess of eggs?" I ask.

"Yes, apparently every year there is a massive excess of eggs here."

I'm floundering now. "Um, how do you have an excess of eggs? Isn't it something that's planned through the number of chooks you choose to have?"

Wendy bursts out laughing. "You know what I mean. I mean yolks. They use the egg whites for food filling and fining of wine, so they have all these yolks left over. Instead of throwing them away, they use them for the tarts."

Yes, I should have known. Wendy often says something other than what she means, which leaves you doing mental gymnastics in attempting to work out the *actual* message. By the time we've cleared this up we've reached the shop. A smile of delight begins to play across my wife's face as she chooses from the myriad of tarts on display. As in the other Portuguese cities, this visit of Wendy's soon becomes a daily ritual. I have no idea how she manages to keep her great figure, just another of her mysterious little qualities.

This morning, after the quaffing of several tarts, we're visiting the Castelo de S. Jorge, or St George's Castle if you're English speaking. It's quite a hike up to the Castle, through winding, narrow and very crowded laneways full of tiny shops, tiny apartments, bars, and cafes. The lanes are cobbled, with stones worn smooth and shiny from centuries of pedestrians. They are also incredibly steep, as are all hills in Lisbon and most of Portugal, so that climbing involves numerous 'breathers' as well as a few slips on the steeper sections.

Added to these challenges is the fact that a large cruise liner docked in the Port early this morning and its disgorged passengers are also making their way *en masse* to the Castle. The colourful, noisy Tuk Tuks are doing a roaring trade, picking up passengers who have indulged too much on their cruise and are finding the going tough. These tiny three-wheel vehicles are basically powered by lawn-mower engines and struggle mightily with the weight of three or four passengers crammed into their seats. The exhaust belches choking, black clouds from their rears as their drivers extract the full 50cc from tiny motors. The drivers lean forward, willing the Tuk Tuk onwards and upwards while the motor screams in protest and passengers look anxious. It's what you call an *experience,* but one no one seems to be enjoying it much.

Finally, after some heavy breathing and a lot of sweat, we're nearing the top, and the queue. The line of people, however, *does* seem to be moving quickly and we're only waiting twenty minutes before we're shown through the large iron gates. I've been amazed at the superbly preserved condition of Portugal's medieval monuments, buildings and walls on this trip. The Castle looming above us is no exception, and standing in its courtyard, you have to be impressed by the architecture and the way it commands a physical and psychological presence. It was obviously designed to protect, but possibly more so, to illustrate the hegemonic reign of the Moors who built it. The Castle was built at about the same time William was conquering Britain and as William demonstrated across that small island, this was a period when the continued success of conquerors was conditional upon their continued demonstration of power. Sustainability required that they strike fear into subjects and potential invaders alike. Large, threatening castles were excellent props.

The actual history of the site can be traced to 700 BCE, when the concepts of multiculturalism and globalisation, even though not labelled as such, were already in full swing. There is evidence that the site was shared in quick succession by Celtic, Iberian, Phoenician, Carthaginian and Greek tribes, and alternated between a meeting place for trade, tribal gatherings and peace deals. It wasn't until the 2nd century BCE that the site was recognised for its strategic potential as a hilltop fortress. Again, different tribes fortified the hill to protect what they thought should be theirs as well as providing a menacing reminder to others of the advantages of fighting from 'above'. Between the 12th and 16th centuries, after they had successfully removed the Moors, several Portuguese Kings decided it was a fitting, *and safe* place to reside and entertain aristocratic friends. The Castle became the pinnacle of elitism, a gathering place that outsiders envied and insiders coveted. Today, it is a rather solid and permanent salute to the richness of Portugal's history and the dark grandeur of medieval architecture. But it also lends itself to commerce, with a museum and gift shop, a restaurant and an exotic bird park. Where once it extracted blood from intruders, now it is the more useful, but perhaps equally transient Euro.

Wendy and I spend a good few hours wandering around the walls, taking in the magical views from the highest points while eating ice-cream purchased from the mobile van in the courtyard. It's a warm day so we seek shade under the large oak trees in the courtyard, watching the crowds enter and leave. There are those who bound in with anticipation, keen to know everything they can about this historical site. There are more commonly the tired and frustrated parents with two or more children who take turns in whinging loudly about their sore feet, run off to discover a stick in the dirt, or ask when it's time to go. Then you have people who are here purely to tick this site off their to-do list. They stride purposefully from one point to the next, snapping several photos at each, taking selfies in front of the more 'appealing' sites, frowning at people who get in their way, and leave again before we've even finished our ice-creams. Finally, you have that peculiar and hard to fathom breed of humans, the teenagers. They arrive in groups, safely detached from any parent but still within sight in case money is required. They giggle, scoff, laugh at indecipherable jokes, take endless selfies, kick dirt and remember nothing of their visit.

We decide it's time to leave these wonders behind and head back to the gates and then the steep descent back through ancient, claustrophobic alleys. By chance, at one of the cross-streets, Wendy spots a large number of people entering a tall building. We trail after them in case they know a short-cut. Well, it is one *heck* of a short-cut, because they're piling into a lift which, it turns out, cuts through the centre of the entire hill, taking you on a vertical trajectory for more than 200 feet. The entrepreneurial spirit of these Portuguese never rests, however, because at the bottom you are deposited right inside the local supermarket. It works a treat. Before we know it, we're perusing the aisles with our lift companions, picking out a selection of goodies for tonight.

The supermarket belongs to the ubiquitous Pino Doce chain. It's one of the dominant players in Portuguese grocery retail. The chain has over four hundred stores throughout the country, ranging in size from local co-ops, to your average pedestrian supermarket, to the massive hypermarkets found in larger cities. Some even have restaurants within, as well as chemists and shoe shops. Pingo Doce is considered the market leader and honestly, it's hard to escape them. They are used by locals and visitors alike as landmarks and meeting spots but also boast such an array of goods that most of your needs can be met under a single roof, from the notorious counters filled with smoked cod and eels that lend the interior that overpoweringly pungent stench, to multiple aisles of wine so cheap that you have to wonder if it should perhaps be called something else. They cater to every need, every type of customer and every price-point.

Seduced

If Lisbon first strikes you as chaotic, brash, grating, and gritty, give it time. Slowly, relentlessly, the city seeps into your bones. You adjust so completely to its rhythm that, rather than grazing your senses, it becomes mesmerizing. You begin to absorb and appreciate its myriad of charms, its mood swings, tenacity and most attractively, its acceptance of all. At night the chaos subsides. Lisbon enters a veritable *wonderland* in which lights of golden yellow, rimmed with brightest white, dark shadows and blueish tinges cast their spell. There is the magical foreshore in its sombre stillness of softly lapping water and yachts rolling sleepily on the swell. The centuries-old buildings bathed in their softest yellow invite you through narrow lanes where locals gather to gossip and pass time. They sip coffee or small glasses of Port, smoke thin acrid smelling cigarettes that glow like fire flies in the darkness.

These seductive, cosy corridors of time let you glimpse another Lisbon, one that stays largely hidden during the chaotic days but is always in the background, the bedrock of this chameleon city. Tiny shops stay open to tempt a final exchange. The Castle above observes all, proudly on its hill casting shadows from its floodlit presence, adding to the quiet embrace of the night. Lisbon at night is a resting giant, quietly preparing itself for the excitement of tomorrow. To walk among its people is to share the mood, to appreciate just how different this city is. The history flows before you, carrying the tumult and tranquillity of so many episodes, of which yours will just be one more. Lisbon is a city apart, a city that challenges you to embrace it, just as it will inevitably embrace you.

****

We are both avid readers so our next stop is a must. Livraria do Simão is argued to be the smallest bookshop in the world, and it's right here in Lisbon. Even in a city of shoebox sized shops, this one is unusual. It's so small, in fact, that only one person at a time can be inside...and that's including the owner. He has to leave the premises while you go in and choose your book, you then take the book out to him, and he steps back in to ring up the sale. And that's because every available inch of the shop is taken up with rows and rows of books – over 4,000 of them crammed into the tightest of spaces. The shop was only opened in 2008 so is certainly not old. But this minute retail space of a mere four-square metres is incredibly successful. I can only imagine that with the number of visitors it receives each day, the owner, having to step out each time, must be one of the fittest retailers in Portugal.

In a city full of bookshops, Lisbon also boasts a bookshop that is the oldest and largest. Opened in 1732 by a French immigrant, it has remained in continuous operation ever since. In its earliest days it housed just 169 books but for the day, was exceedingly well stocked. The eighteenth century was an age when books were rare. Reading, in some quarters, was frowned upon as a source of radical thoughts and ideas which could lead the unwary astray if not monitored carefully. What's more, because of their limited production, books tended to be prohibitively expensive. Those who *could* afford them and could read well enough to understand more than a street sign would, because of the cost, limit themselves to two or three, reading them over and over again.

From the 1940s, however, the shop expanded rapidly and even installed its own printing press to reduce costs and increase supply. The innovation allowed the shop to vastly improve its economies of scale, eventually printing its own titles for distribution and allowing the owners to enter the lucrative publishing business. By the end of the 1940s the bookshop became the largest distributor of foreign books in the world, a development that would sustain its success for the generations to come. It now sits proudly in the

Guinness Book of Records and its name – *Bertrand* – commands an empire of over fifty bookstores. More importantly, it has secured its position as a beacon of light in the renaissance of Portuguese literature.

****

Back to front

After a restless sleep in our less than salubrious attic, we awake to a glorious morning with the view from our window bright and dazzling. The ocean is a vast shimmer of silver, blindingly so. The sky is clear, expansive and blue, promising another gorgeous day. The city is still shaking off its slumber, with a smattering of people up and moving about. One or two shorefront cafes below us creak open their shutters and place the first chairs on the sidewalk. Lisbon prepares for another day. We squeeze into the bathroom, try to ignore the encroaching mould, coax the anaemic shower, dress and step out into the early stillness, enjoying relative solitude before the daily crowds emerge.

First stop is the Millennium bcp Foundation. This is the site of one of Lisbon's banks but when renovated in the early 1990s, a substantial number of archaeological ruins and remains were uncovered. They spanned more than 2,500 years of the city's history and harbour a wealth of historical knowledge that we are pretty keen to find out about. Apparently, you can view remains from seven distinct periods, including the Ibero-Punic, Roman, Visigoth, Moorish, Medieval, Renaissance and Pombaline phases. The first and last of these phases I hadn't even heard of, so my excitement levels are up. The Museum is about a ten-minute walk down into the centre of the city with its utilitarian Pomabline style architecture. This architectural style arose after the 1755 earthquake, which devastated most of Lisbon with the exception of the Alfama. It was the brain child of an engineer - Marquês de Pombal - and reflects his pragmatic, secular and importantly, anti-seismic approach.

Crossing the city praça is an experience in itself. It is huge in scale, already thronged with locals and day-trippers alike but it's the almost Parisian style which grabs your attention. There are coffee shops and restaurants, boutique fashion shops and the transients trying to tempt you with their latest commercial 'amusement'.

As we navigate the streets beyond, the rhythm of the city is changing again, accelerating, moving up a gear. Ordering two take-away coffees, we front up to the unassuming Museum's door, only to find it firmly locked. The advertised times on the door suggest it shouldn't be. We decide to sit in the square and drink our coffees while waiting for what is hopefully, a tardy employee to open. Twenty-minutes later Wendy tries the door again but it's still locked and there's no sign of light or life in the alcove just inside. We're mystified.

Plan B is to visit the large foreshore plaza where politicians have strategically constructed their government buildings to take full advantage of the most beautiful part of the city. Praça do Comerécio is large, open and exceptionally beautiful. Ornate fountains, a tree-lined perimeter and open, heavily patterned flooring distinguish it markedly from its surroundings. But it also opens onto the seafront, providing a wide, open vista with spectacular views of the great Atlantic Ocean. Groups of tourists take photos of the fountains, the government buildings and statues and, most of all, each other.

The Praça once acted as entree to the vast trading port that catapulted Lisbon and therefore Portugal into the busiest, most profitable, and influential trading centre the world had ever known. For several centuries Portugal extracted much of its wealth from this single grand Praça, but in return, it also sent forth numerous men of vision and talent to explore the unknown world. For much of the 15th, 16th and even 17th centuries, Lisbon became the epicentre of an exploration empire that set the world on fire with the wonder of discovery. This was a new age of circumnavigation, and Portugal was its beacon at one stage, claiming 'ownership' of more than half the New World. Explorers such as Bartolomeu Dias and Vasco de Gama, Ferdinand Magellan, Francisco Pizarro and Christopher Columbus brought colonies from North and South America, Africa and Asia into Portugal's global orbit. They also sowed the seeds of Portuguese culture and Catholicism within much of the New World, thus ensuring further hegemony.

Deciding to take our lunch in a small, quaint little park above the city, Wendy leads the way through more winding lanes and steep hills, but this time, we head for our sneaky little elevator, half way up. Alighting at the top, it's only a few hundred metres to the park. Around the next corner, we come across a short line of fellows waiting outside a small, green stall. "Will you look at that," Wendy exclaims. "It's an open-air men's urinal." There, in the middle of the lane, in full view of the throngs of people walking up and down this hill is a small, dark green urinal with two-foot-high metal sheeting covering what the designers consider the average height of a man's modesty. I like the novelty of relieving myself in one of these open-air units, so join the queue. Wendy is looking carefully at the stall, then at me, then back at the stall.

"Darling," she says quietly, "There is no way you are using that stall."

"Why? Don't be such a Puritan."

"It has nothing to do with being a Puritan. Just look at the height of the metal sheeting and then look at yourself. Remember, you are, well... short. You will literally be urinating in front of everyone because that sheeting won't even begin to cover you."

I line myself up and quickly decide that the novelty has already worn off.

We arrive at the park, find ourselves a bench under a large Jacaranda tree and settle in to eat packed sandwiches. Our bench is at the very edge of the park with the most idyllic views of the entire city below and the crystal blue of the Atlantic beyond that. A five-star restaurant couldn't offer better views. Even though the park is small, it's isolated and removed from the hustle of the city just a hundred yards away. It is quiet, serene, a perfect oasis of calm. I am just suggesting to Wendy that we might sit and relax for an hour or so when the park warden with his bright orange fluorescent jacket approaches and gruffly advises that we must leave now.

Wendy fixes him with one of her measured stares and calmly asks, "Oh, why is that?"

"I close the park now so I can sleep."

"Can't you just sleep with the park open?" Wendy asks.

"No, you must leave now. I go home to sleep." He starts waving his arms at us to get up and follow him out. And so concludes our idyllic retreat, far earlier than we wanted. Perhaps the five-star restaurant would have been better after all.

There's nothing for it but to extend our exploration several blocks in the other direction and visit the famous Águas Livres Aqueduct alongside the Avenue Ceuta. I'm glad we did. Standing before us is a magnificent Baroque architectural wonder. It towers over the city below, dwarfing unit blocks, roads, shops and other bridges. It's huge. Spanning a valley with a busy road running through its great arches, its sheer size is brought into scale by the tiny cars that race underneath like toys in a child's playground. Each of the arches is enormous in its own right, shaped like the stain-glassed windows in a cathedral but far more enthralling. Placed at regular intervals along the aqueduct's top are small watch towers and today, the brave can walk where water once flowed, but the height and the busy road below are a little too much for us today.

The aqueduct was commissioned by King Dom João V and built over a period of almost seventy years from 1731 to 1799. As part of the architectural renaissance sweeping the world at this time, the Águas Livres Aqueduct stands proudly as one of Portugal's finest achievements. It was also the last classical aqueduct to be built anywhere in the world. It spans an incredible thirty-six miles and was used to transport vital water between the major settlements of Lisbon, Amadora, Oeiras, Odivelas and Sintra, where it not only quenched the thirst of city inhabitants but also their thirsty croplands. Following the same route as the original Roman aqueduct, it borrowed heavily from that empire of engineering and design marvels, with a gravity fed system and Roman arches built with the type of precision that we find hard to match today.

There is a darker side to this aqueduct, however. In the 1800s, forty years after its final phase of construction, it became the gruesome burial place of seventy-six unfortunate Lisbon souls. The 1840s, you see, witnessed the emergence of Portugal's most notorious and deadly serial killer and he lived right here in Lisbon. Alves, a young man of nineteen was sent from his country home to Lisbon to gain some work. Here, he took up with an older Innkeeper by the name of Maria Gertrudes and a rather steamy relationship developed. It is not known why, but many of the locals blame this relationship for Alves' change of personality and an unpleasant partiality for all things dead.

Soon after he met Maria, he began to warm to the idea of killing people. He would lay in wait down by the aqueduct on dark nights, ready to snare any unwary passer-by. He would rob them of their money and jewellery, then march them to the top of the aqueduct from which he would push them to their death, some sixty metres (196 feet) below. This way, he hoped that their deaths would be passed off as suicide, removing him from any suspicion. Perhaps a good idea, except that after a dozen or so of these deaths, the authorities began to have doubts about the sheer number of people who suddenly wanted to end their own lives, all from the same spot. His luck came to an abrupt end when Maria's own daughter decided she'd had enough and reported her mother and Alves to the courts. Maria was sent into lifelong exile and Alves was executed. And so ended one of the darkest chapters in Lisbon's history.

****

Incongruence

Back to daylight and more innocent issues; there are two great anomalies that repeatedly strike me throughout Portugal. The first is the Portuguese penchant for coffee. Apart from them introducing the notion of tea drinking to Britain, they also introduced coffee to much of the world. Portugal first got hold of the coffee bean in about 1730, when its leaders discovered the commercial importance it played next door in French Guiana. The Governor of that state, however, refused to allow secrets of this liquid goldmine to be passed on to any, let alone a country he considered a rival. So one of the wily Portuguese diplomats resorted to an age-old strategy of gaining access by seducing the Governor's wife. She fell in love with him, and as a parting gift, smuggled some of her husband's famous coffee beans to his entourage.

Over the following decades, the Portuguese adapted the bean to their growing conditions and ended up with a product that, as I have mentioned earlier, is rather special. Yet, as is so often the case, the early Portuguese themselves did not take to the product. In fact, they made a point of shunning the delicious concoction, leaving only the poorest of the country to consume it on a daily basis. And the poor consumed it because it was the only beverage they could afford. So a brew fit for a king, and secured in such a precarious way by kings, was seen as acceptable only to the poorest of their subjects. It has only been quite recently that tastes and culture have changed to an extent that coffee has become part of the daily ritual for *all* Portuguese citizens. To be fair, however, they are certainly making up for lost time.

The other issue that confounds me now that we have travelled through a good part of the country, is their cork. The Portuguese refer to this product as "gold grown on a tree". Cork began its utilitarian life in the 3rd century BCE, when it joined hands with wine to provide the perfect, organic bottle seal. But in Portugal, particularly, cork has become an empire in itself. It is now also used in shoes, thermal insulation, pollution absorption mats, tiles, even handbags and purses. Here, the hot, often dry Mediterranean climate suits it perfectly. Its compressibility, together with its water-proof and fire-retardant properties mean that apart from sealing millions of wine bottles worldwide, its demand is also increasing in a vast array of other industries. And for these reasons, Portugal is the largest cork producer and exporter in the world. The great beauty in growing cork, is sustainability, as no tree ever needs to be cut down for its production; it is merely stripped of its bark every eight or nine years and regenerates ready to be stripped again. If you make the mistake of asking any Portuguese about cork, they will bombard you for far longer than you'd like with all its possible benefits.

But here's the thing; despite its wonderful qualities and its organic, sustainable, next-to-Godliness status, the cork I come across here in its home country, is nothing short of rubbish. I have pulled many a wine cork in my time, but far too frequently, when I pull a wine cork in Portugal it either snaps in two or disintegrates into a crumbling mess before I get it half-way out of the bottle. I can only conclude that they export the highest quality cork to the rest of the world and keep the discarded off-cuts for themselves.

Cisterns and tour guides

This afternoon, Wendy and I are booked in on one of the more authentic city tours, conducted by volunteer residents who seem to know an awful lot about their city. We are to meet back down at the Praça do Comerécio, from where the three-hour tour begins and we only have about seven minutes to get there. After power-walking through laneways, dead-end alleys and along busy streets, Wendy thinks she might know a shortcut. I have to say, that apart from finding the lift, our shortcuts over the years have been nothing short of disastrous. I still have very bad memories from last year when walking the 102-mile Cotswold Way in England, each so-called shortcut would add several miles to a day's walk and often lead us into rather unfortunate situations. But still, we have this idea that the next one will be different. Wendy is always keen to try and for reasons I still can't fathom, I'm always keen to follow.

Today, Wendy's 'research-on-the-go' has led her to believe that if we cut across the hill instead of taking the natural route down, we'll somehow slice a good five minutes off the trip. Because my navigation skills are non-existent, I'm happy enough to believe her. The first attempt leads into a dead-end. We back track and try another laneway which eventually leads up the hill, the opposite direction to where we want to be heading. Deciding to cut our losses, we navigate our way back to the original route and break into a jog. Rounding the very first bend we're confronted by an entire family carrying a toilet. That's right. They're ambling along as if it's the most normal thing in the world. The father is carrying the heavy toilet bowl, the wife is carrying the cistern, and their small daughter is carrying the toilet lid, swinging it above her head in her own private game. No-one else on the street seems to be taking any notice but Wendy and I are mesmerised. It is such a quintessential element of this city's delightfully unaffected and unstudied character.

Recovering from the travelling toilet bowl, we belatedly arrive at the tour's starting point just as the group is moving off. Hurriedly, we introduce ourselves to the guide, apologise for our tardiness, and join with the other ten or so enthusiasts. Apart from missing the introductory spiel, we learn a great deal on the tour. I highly recommend to anyone visiting places for the first time to look up these local (non-tourist) historic or city tours and book yourself in. Dedicated and knowledgeable volunteers set aside several hours to lead you through cultural and historical enclaves off the tourist map, places you wouldn't come across in your guidebook. In addition to the well-known historical events and artefacts, you'll learn about the stories of ordinary people who have lived, worked and contributed to the city's evolution. It is a marvellous overview.

A curse on your city

Foremost in the tour's insights was the significant obstacles Lisbon overcame to become one of Europe's most vibrant and enlightened cities. Although the city was founded a full four centuries before Rome, around 1200BC, it spent many centuries mired in invasion and political/religious turmoil before it could emerge into a flourishing trading hub.

But even more stifling than these disruptions, according to our guide, were two profound impacts. The first was the plague, or Black Death, that struck Europe with brutal disregard in the 1350s and decimated almost half the population over the next decade. It is difficult for us today, to comprehend the scale and devastation of this outbreak, and the long-term practical and psychological impacts it had on all those it touched. Like Italy, the UK, Germany, France and Spain, Portugal was reduced to a skeletal shadow of what it had once been. Families, businesses, trade, agriculture, manufacture, indeed the march of civilisation, was reduced to rubble in a few short years, not to recover for decades and in some areas, not at all. For some time, in fact, much of Europe returned to the Dark Ages, where all progress, all endeavour ground to a halt, as whole societies came to terms with the utter devastation that scarred their outlook for generations to come. But this was not specific to Portugal. What was far more distinctive, was the combination of religious developments that would accompany and follow this natural disaster.

These revolved around the rise of the Jesuits and Dominicans. Following the 'reconquest' in which the Moors were defeated and largely evicted, the Church's power escalated dramatically. Its cultural reach and wealth increased in line with its political influence and throughout the entire medieval period, as the saying goes, "To be Portuguese was to be Catholic". Jesuit and Dominican friars were the living, breathing embodiment of this power, increasingly ruling their flocks with an iron fist. Social practices, public behaviour, personal beliefs, and even conduct within the confines of the home, were regulated with the most draconian of codes. There was no room for deviation, no escape from the Church's expectations and demands. What you learnt, how you learnt it, what you did with your spare time, how you dressed and conversed, how and when you prayed, how you lived your daily life were directed and monitored by your religious superiors.

And so, as you might imagine, the dramatic limits on personal freedom of thought and action, in turn suppressed progress as a civilisation. Ultimately, the rigidity of these codes and the accompanying paranoia and greed of the medieval church culminated in the Portuguese Inquisition.

Emerging as an unstoppable force in the 1530s and spanning almost three centuries, this Inquisition represents what is possibly Portugal's darkest hour. The paranoia focused on the perceived heretical thoughts and practices arising within the Church's flock and the need to stamp them out with increasing ferocity. But it was also the result, as in Spain, of the Church's pervasive greed at the time. You see, the majority of the poor sods targeted in this Inquisition, were, as is usual in such persecutions, the Jews. The Church did not trust that their conversion to Catholicism was authentic, or more accurately, it was convenient to believe it wasn't authentic. And that's because the Jewish population in Portugal, as elsewhere, was highly successful at money-changing, trade and commerce. They accumulated substantial wealth, vastly disproportionate to their population numbers. The medieval Catholic Church wanted that wealth. The means of getting it were to confiscate any person's financial assets if they were convicted of heresy. It just so happens that the majority of the 40,000 who were convicted of heresy were of Jewish origin.

The broader, lasting consequences of these developments became most apparent in the late 1600s and 1700s when, beginning in Italy and then rippling throughout the rest of Europe, the medieval period gave way to a new era of enlightenment and creativity. The Renaissance swiftly followed, with great leaps forward in literature, art, architecture, astronomy, and scientific thought. But this wave of liberalisation and progress, this lifting of the darkened veil, bypassed the Portuguese. Their world remained firmly under that veil, firmly within the grasp of the Church, firmly prohibited from exploring new, secular knowledge. It was a darkness which would continue to handicap Portugal's own 'enlightenment' for generations.

You wouldn't, however, guess this walking through Lisbon today. And this morning tour, focusing on cultural centres, bookshops, art galleries, street art, the vibrant city centre and eclectic infusions of fashion and food demonstrates just how enlightened and cosmopolitan the city has become. I should also point out that the poetic justice of this delayed enlightenment was demonstrated exquisitely during the Second World War, with many Portuguese citizens working feverishly in the underground movement on the covert extraction of Jews from Germany and Hungary. It was an illumination that allowed this persecuted race to rebuild with at least some of the hope that had been denied them for so long.

Toward the end of the tour I mention to the guide the trouble we had getting into the Roman Museum. He looks perplexed. "It is always open, every day it's open. Here I'll take you now, it's just around the corner". He leads us to a large, ornate door we haven't seen before. "Here it is, open see?" I explain that this isn't the door we've been trying over and over again. He frowns, then laughs and says, "You must have gone to the back. It's always locked. This is the front door." Wendy and I just look at each, shake our heads at our stupidity, and thank him. Of course, by now we have missed the boat so to speak, because in less than an hour we're heading to Belém, on the outskirts of Lisbon, and home to Jerónimos Monastry.

****

On our walk to the bus station for the journey to Belém, Wendy spots a "Doll Hospital" on the other side of the street. This is a first. Apparently, it's the world's oldest doll hospital. Set up in the Praça da Figueira of Lisbon in 1830, it specialises in body parts, repairs, and rejuvenation. But more surprisingly, there's a four-month waiting list to get your doll admitted. That's longer than many human hospitals. The list of casualties is quite macabre. There are missing eyes, so many that you begin to wonder just what the owners do with them. There are mutilated arms, amputated limbs, caved in heads, neat incisions that run the length of the stomach (obviously home-based operations that have gone wrong) bitten-off noses, even missing lips. It gives you a whole new perspective on domestic violence. When you consider that a large percentage of the hospital's customers are adults and the dolls are from their own collection, you wonder what people get up to in the privacy of their own home, but don't dwell on it too long.

The dolls are all tagged with their date of arrival, the ailments from which they are suffering, and the expected length of stay in hospital. Just like their human equivalents, the nasty surprise of cost is kept until release. The hospital is so busy that four 'surgeons' are on duty at any one time, working long hours and even weekends to keep up with the demand. Finally, after an exorbitant sum of money is handed over, the dolls are ready to be released back into their owner's care for more torture and punishment.

Monasteries, pastries and queues

On what turns out to be our fifty-minute, crowded tram ride to Belém, we're told to expect more crowds once we reach our destination. Almost everyone who comes to Lisbon - visitors, tourists, international workers and those deposited daily by the giant cruise ships - will, at some stage, descend on Belém. It's a magnet. Like most others on this tram, Wendy and I are heading to Jerónimos Monastery. It is only one, however, of the many attractions this city-within-a-city boasts. There is Belém Tower located *in* the water rather than simply the waterfront, various museums, Pastéis de Belémé, and Ajuda Palace, to name a few. When we alight from our tram, we realise that today, everyone has had the same idea as us. In fact, I think the throngs of visitors have the same idea every day. The plaza into which we're deposited is a sea of humanity. I want to turn and hop back on the tram, but Wendy gives me one of her *looks*.

There are people coming at us from all angles, much the same as traffic in Rome. We're bumped, elbowed, pushed, have our feet trampled by selfie-taking teenagers, squawked at by irritable children being dragged by frustrated parents, and generally jolted through the congested plaza. I'm hating it already but Wendy now has a firm grip on my arm and is leading me to the Monastery and what I realise with horror, is a queue that snakes its way around the building's entire perimeter, and then along a side street for as far as the eye can see.

The first thing to understand about Jerónimos Monastery, which was built under the orders of King Manuel I in the early 1500s, is that it wasn't all about religion. It was more about showing Portugal's wealth and power to the world. Religion was secondary. This was the great Age of Discovery for Portugal, the era when its explorers and merchants went abroad to uncover and extract vast amounts of wealth from new lands. I suppose the most obvious illustration of this in Belém is that the great explorer Vasco Da Gama was actually buried in this Monastery, forever linking it to Portugal's maritime empire. But Da Gama also continued the exploration after death. You see his body was first buried in the St. Francis Church, Fort Kochi, in India. Vandals, however, used this area and particularly the church as an area to test their destructive skills and after a little time, it was decided that there was too much risk in leaving Da Gama's body entombed there. It was exhumed and shipped along one of his favourite sea routes back to Portugal to be buried with all the fanfare of his celebrity status in Lisbon. The problem is that there are persistent rumours that unofficially, his body was exhumed and spirited away years before the official exhumation and that, to save face, the Indian authorities substituted some other poor devil's body and pretended it was Da Gama. In the days before DNA and other forensic testing, it was a bit hard to tell the difference, so we will never know who is actually buried in the Monastery.

What the second burial of Da Gama in Lisbon *did* do, was to create a massive income flow for the Monastery through a dramatic rise in the number of visitors who wanted to see the explorer's final resting place. From commoners, to local aristocrats to visiting royalty, all came and were prepared to pay for the privilege. Perhaps this deft move was simply orchestrated by those astute monks as another source of income. The site does, however, also host the tombs of Maria of Aragon and Queen Catherine of Hapsburg, linking it to European royalty and raising its own heritage status to qualify under OECD guidelines and prompting the King of Portugal to declare it "a very special place".

The Monastery itself is vast, imposing and impressive indeed. It was home to monks for much of its life, from the Order of Saint

Jerome, and is a testament to the way these 'bastions of poverty' liked to indulge themselves. The building is magnificent but also slightly obscene in its sheer opulence, a stark symbol of the enormous gulf between the cloistered religious orders and the poverty-stricken people they ruled.

What isn't so magnificent, is the queue we must join simply to purchase our ticket for the next queue to enter the Monastery. All-in-all, we spend more than two hours between the ticket office and the Monastery's queue, standing in the beating sun while Gypsies in their dozens, pester us all to buy their wares. They are relentless. If you so much as glance in their direction they are on to you, refusing "No" for an answer. By the time we enter the actual building, we're exhausted. And, just when we're inside and ready at last to wander through this spectacle, Wendy announces the fact that she needs another toilet break. I find a secluded position behind one of the pillars to wait through the lengthy delay.

Apart from the ostentatious sculptures, paintings, statues and marble floors, there are no less than twelve Confessionals where the Monastery's monks would regularly listen to the sins of poor pilgrims. Given the indulgent lives these monks lived, I can't help but think it might have been more productive the other way around. After another two hours spent battling crowds *inside* the Monastery, we come away wondering why so much fuss is made about this structure. Yes, it is vast and magnificent in its own way, but to us, it is really one giant display of indulgence.

Of less celebrity, but more interest to us is the Belém Tower, or Tower of St Vincent that sits across the other side of the plaza, knee-deep in in the Tagus River. Built of thick, grey granite the Tower resembles a major turret and entranceway to a medieval castle. It would have been imposing in its day, particularly with its position stretching from the shore into the actual River. This Tower was a central feature of Portugal's Age of Discovery and, again a symbol of the country's maritime success. The meeting of the Tagus and the sea at this point represents Lisbon's gateway, the place where its sea power flowed to and from. It was also the first gateway of many visitors to Lisbon, royals, aristocrats, great merchants, and others of a more hostile nature. The public of the day was told that the Tower was fortressed, to protect Lisbon from any invasion or simple incursion. It was completely inadequate for such a task, in reality constructed to show friends and foes alike just how powerful Portugal had become – a grand boast and a thinly veiled warning all in one. It worked. If on your own tour you must choose between the Monastery and this Tower, I would recommend the latter.

But one final stop before we leave this over-crowded city-within-a-city – the Pastéis de Belém. At Wendy's insistence, we make our way to the most famous Portuguese tart shop in the world, where these little custard delicacies have been in production since 1837. The monks from up the hill at the Monastery were, once again, responsible for the tart's (pastel de natas) initial production and their popularity has increased at a highly lucrative rate ever since. Like many other traditions and practices among the monks, the recipe for these tarts has remained a tightly held secret to which only a handful of people have access. All pastel de natas are still handmade with strict quality control. The shop remains Lisbon's number one tourist attraction year after year, and judging by the size of the queue as we turn the corner, that's a claim I would not dispute.

Snaking from its doorway is the beginning of a human tide that runs the length of the entire street, blocking the entrance to a dozen other shops as people inch forward in their quest to participate in culinary history. Wendy joins the back of the queue but since I can't eat these seductive little morsels anyway, I stand away, taking photos of the crowds and the shop before heading in to see what happens in the heart of the empire.

Once inside, customers are spread ten-deep at the counter. They order and pay at one end, then move along to join another queue to collect their prizes. I count twelve staff behind the counter, taking orders, packing and serving the tarts. I can only imagine the number of staff behind the scenes actually baking them. The entire operation runs like a well-oiled clock. Every staff member knows exactly what they are doing. No-one is giving instructions, no-one is asking questions. They are all just working on their own specific function, as they have probably been doing for years.

Because of the shop's reputation, the tarts here are more expensive than the hundreds of other tart shops across the country. My perennial interest in finance takes over and I begin doing a rough calculation per customer. I estimate that on average, each customer is spending roughly €10. When I extrapolate this figure across the number of customers in the shop and lining the street, my mind begins to whirl. I suspect that with the number of staff serving, they are raking in around €2,000-2,500 per hour. Then I take the easier way and research the figures. I have dramatically underestimated. Currently, this little shop sells more than 20,000 pastel de natas a day and at €4 per tart, that's a very handy €80,000 per day in takings. This goes on all day, every day. Not a bad enterprise at all and knowing those wily monks, they are probably still collecting royalties on the original recipe.

Eventually, Wendy makes it into the shop, receives her tarts and we head back to the tram station for our return to Lisbon proper. Two dilapidated police cars pass with sirens blaring and lights flashing. They're obviously in a hurry, but the age of their cars means they are struggling to pick up a decent speed. The police cars in Portugal, I have noticed, are a random collection of variously aged cars (mostly old) some with rust, usually dirty, and often not in the best repair. We have seen ten-year-old Toyotas, Fiats, Mitsubishis, the small VW Polo, and pre-2000 Nissans. Apparently, there is one Audi R8 pursuit car for the entire force, so as long as criminals know roughly where that car is touring, they can pretty safely bet on getting away. I'm not sure why there is such a rag-tag collection but I can't help thinking that these old cars, of different colours, different ages and different states of repair don't do a whole lot for the image and reputation of the Portuguese police. In fact, as most of them pass, you find yourself having a quiet chuckle. I wonder how many crooks they nab in an average day?

From chaos to serenity with a bit of dyslexia

We arise early. Yesterday was our last in the intriguing, beguiling, wonderfully chaotic city of Lisbon. This morning we're heading back down the oh so steep lane from our apartment to Lisbon's train station (or one of several major ones), where we are to embark on our next leg of the journey - the terribly old city of 'Obidos, one hour by car, two and a half by train. At the entrance to the station there stands an iconic statue of King Sebastion, that locals and visitors alike have marvelled at for the past 126 years. It is one of the key symbols of Lisbon. Shortly after we left Portugal, we read that an over-enthusiastic tourist, in need of yet another selfie, had decided it would be a good idea to climb the statue for a unique shot. Of course, the entire statue collapsed with the tourist perched on top, effectively destroying more than a century of Lisbon's history and memories. You just have to love this age of selfies.

Our departure from the apartment had been a frantic one. We had dawdled through our breakfast, showered at the mercy of a by now, thoroughly fatigued water supply, and packed, while sipping extra coffees and admiring the morning views. Wendy had looked at her watch mid-pack and given a yelp. According to her interpretation of the timetable, we only had fifteen minutes before our train departed. Ramming the last remnants of clothing into cases, rushing around the apartment (a very short distance) to check we hadn't left anything behind, we grabbed jackets, wallets and phones and headed for the door. After a rather precarious trot down our steep lane with bags bouncing behind, we arrived at the station severely out of breath. Wendy rushed up to the counter to purchase tickets and on the way back, happened to glance up at the station clock, then looked at her ticket. Immediately, I saw a very sheepish look wash over her face followed by an even more sheepish glance at me. Her pace slowed and as she approached, she simply said "Uh oh." I already knew what was coming but asked anyway.

“Well,” she began, “I was sure the timetable showed our train leaving at 10.am but the ticket says 11.30am. I think the timetable must be wrong.” With that she pulled it out of her bag and checked. “Oh,... maybe I read it wrongly.” I just sighed, silently cursing her little problem with numbers. So now we had to entertain ourselves for another ninety minutes in a train station.

Óbidos... Medieval Magic

After too long, our train shunts into the platform and an announcement tells us it will be departing soon. It's another relic from the 1930s with all the age-related issues. We select our seat, pull out kindles and settle in for the next few hours. A couple of minutes before we are set to leave, six young fellows with bicycles clamber into our carriage and set themselves and their bikes up in the seats opposite. It turns out that they all attend university in the UK, and are here on break to cycle around Portugal. The six of them are geared up in full cycling clothes, helmets, drink bottles and gloves. But when I ask how long they've been cycling, four of them admit it's their first time on a bike.

They are yet to do their first day's riding in Portugal. I'm thinking that cycling around a country, even as small as Portugal, for your first time on two wheels is a brave display of confidence indeed. I'm imagining their legs and backsides will be letting them know just how brave they are by tonight. I smile and wish them luck. They are full of adrenaline and loud, excitable talk, although I have to say, they *do* seem a lot keener on talking to Wendy than to me.

Their starting point also happens to be our destination, Óbidos, except they have no idea where they'll be staying overnight, or exactly where they'll cycle to tomorrow. Ah, the carefree planning of the young.

Apart from listening to the chatter of the young adventurers and sharing in some of their jokes, the trip is fairly uneventful. There is, however, a significant change in the weather after the first hour. As we continue to head north, the sky darkens, ominously so, with great black clouds building at an alarming rate. Before much longer, these same clouds have burst and are emptying their contents in torrents across the landscape. Daylight is fading fast, way before nightfall, turning uniformly grey and dank with a thick, enveloping mist billowing in. In no time the surrounding landscape has disappeared. Water runs off the carriage roof in rivers, pooling at the side of the tracks. The mood in our carriage is also darkening as we all stare forlornly at our deteriorating day. I glance across at the despondent bicyclists. Worried looks creep across their faces. They must be wondering what Plan B is.

The train conductor strolls through our carriage, smiles and announces to each of us that the next stop is 'Obidos. If anything, the weather is now even worse, with strong winds buffeting the train and bending trees into unnatural angles. Fortunately, our Airbnb host has organised a taxi to pick us up at the station. The cyclists are not so lucky. Silence hangs over the carriage as they begin attending to their bikes and arranging their helmets in a most dejected way. I attempt to say something optimistic about the weather improving tomorrow but it falls flat. Wendy wishes them good luck as we collect our bags and move towards the door.

At last the train shudders and slows, then stops alongside what the sign tells us is 'Obidos station. There is only a short, crumbling platform to meet us. The station house is deserted and derelict. Paint has long left its exterior, there is no-one in attendance and long grass grows through platform cracks and broken floorboards in the waiting room. Not the most welcoming sight to a new destination. The young fellows now have their wet weather gear firmly attached, buttoned up to the chin, as they drag their bikes off the train and call a cheerless goodbye to us. Wendy gives a sympathetic smile as we wish them luck once again. Fortunately for us, a black taxi is waiting outside the station and, as we approach, a cheery driver jumps out with an upbeat, "Ullo" to help with the bags. He apologises for the weather and allays our fears by volunteering that the ancient village of 'Obidos is nothing like the train station.

In a very short time, our enthusiastic, talkative, driver delivers us into the walled village itself. He's forced to park in a steeply inclined, cobbled and slippery parking area two hundred feet from our apartment. Our 'street' is so narrow that driving in isn't an option. Miraculously, however, the rain is already easing off, with breaks in the clouds and tiniest hints of blue sky beyond. It had looked as though it might be settling in for several days, but we've found that trying to predict the weather here is akin to the *dark arts*.

Our first reaction in seeing this village is that it must be the TV setting for a medieval mystery. The entire *centro storico* is encircled by centuries-old fortified walls that have to be at least three feet in width and stretch roughly thirty feet in height. They are of a permanence that will still be here in another thousand years. The village proper (located within the walls) is perched atop one of 'Obidos's highest hills with extensive views in every direction, a key requisite of any successful medieval village. The remainder of the village, the newer section, spreads away below into the surrounding valley, but if you visit here, I highly recommend staying within the historic walls.

'Obidos was founded in AD 734, the earliest twinkling of the medieval period or, what is commonly referred to as the Dark Ages. The architectural style of this period is quite different to that of the latter Middle Ages. It is a more insular, dark, rather unimaginative style that I suppose, reflects its dark period. It was labelled as the pre-Romanesque Iberian style, introduced largely by the Visigoths and designed purely for permanence and protection, not aesthetic expression. My guess is that in 'Obidos not much has changed. You feel that you could wind the clock back by centuries and the scene greeting you would be very similar to the one confronting us today.

The tenements and apartments are crammed together, creating solid walls that line the narrow, cobbled laneways. They lean at odd angles facing their duplicates opposite, the tenants within talking distance of each other, each on intimate terms with every other soul in their street. The lanes are organised in roughly concentric spirals towards the centre of the village and the top of the hill. This was a common design of the times, allowing commanding views towards an approaching enemy and offering increased protection of royalty and religious orders at the centre. The original praca is located in the centre of the village, still hosting markets and musicians and sloping unevenly into a cartwheel of lanes leading down to tiny shops and bars and more ancient terraces.

There is a common misconception that Celtish tribes originated in Switzerland and spread out across Europe, but in fact, it was right here in the Iberian Peninsula. 'Obidos was one of many Portuguese villages and towns they settled, before being overrun by the Visigoths and later, the Moors. But the Celts were only one of many races to put down roots in this area. Today, there are clear reminders of each culture that came and occupied, leaving their buildings, their customs and their wealth of archaeological remains.

Much, much earlier, the village had been fought over almost continuously by competing tribes of the Mesolithic period some 9,000 years ago. Some 4,000 years after that, Neolithic farmers settled the area, claiming the fertile land for their own and slowly replacing the hunter gatherers that had roamed across the region before them. Finally, the Roman invasion, followed by the constructive advance of the Moors, left us with largely what we see today. One of the starkest reminders is the original pillory that still stands in the centre of town. It was used by both Romans and Moors, who led their local criminals here to be humiliated and brutally punished, providing crude entertainment for the village folk before being led off to prison.

Into the portal

Our apartment is at the top of the street, opposite the most spectacular veneer of lilac wisteria, in full flower, stretching from one laneway to the next. Wisteria is Wendy's favourite flower and she's almost beside herself with excitement, snapping photos from every angle. I knock at a red wooden door of a beautifully restored façade. We hear an elderly, female voice inside bark out an instruction in Portuguese and moments later, the door swings in and the beaming face of our host greets us. With a smile stretching across his handsome face, he leans forward and in one movement, sweeps both of us inside. God, I hope this is the right place. “Ollo, Ollo!” he booms. “Welcome to your apartment”. Wendy and I smile back as he hauls us across the narrow foyer and up the stairs. “My mother lives downstairs in her own apartment,” he says. “Ignore her, she will not bother you. She is ninety”. At the top of the stairs, our apartment opens up into a spacious, immaculately kept, traditional Portuguese space. There is a large kitchen, a rustic living area with fireplace, two bedrooms, a smallish bathroom, and a long hallway running the length of the apartment, all with exceptionally high ceilings. It's wonderful. “Come,” he says, “I show you the best part”. With that, he hurries us through a centuries-old wooden door, into a glorious, sun-soaked backyard. The yard is ringed by half a dozen mature orange and lemon trees, has a little love seat in the centre, and its own mini stone wall encircling it, almost a replica of the village's. From here, you look up to the village wall looming above you, and down across the rest of 'Obidos. It is an utterly private space, and what a treat it is.

After providing us with more information about the apartment and the village than we can hope to absorb, as well as detailed instructions on how to successfully light the fire without too much smoke, our energetic host turns, bounds down the stairs and is gone. He had even offered to run us into the new part of town to do grocery shopping each day, but given it was only a twenty-minute walk we thought this was being overly generous. Wendy and I turn to each other and smile. Instantly, we have a really good feeling about this place and know we'll enjoy our time. "What a lovely fellow," Wendy enthuses. I agree, but suspect the fellow's looks may have a lot to do with her opinion. I say as much and Wendy tells me not to be so silly, while turning a shade of beetroot. We unload our bags and set off to explore this ancient wonderland.

'Obidos is small, with a mere 3,100 souls, only fifty of which live inside the original walls. So before 11.am when the tourists show up each day, and after 4.pm, when they leave, you have this glorious Gothic village to yourself. It's late afternoon now, and the laneways are eerily quiet. We wander at leisure, taking in the sights and smells, marvelling at the almost complete preservation of more than a thousand years of history. In the main praca, with narrow lanes stretching tentacle-like from its perimeter, you have the ubiquitous tourist shops, selling postcards, Ginja, port, t-shirts and other disposable trinkets, but you also have the traditional cafes and bars that have been plying their trade for generations. Some of these are large and cavernous, others mere holes in the wall into which no more than three tables fit.

****

No matter where you look, the walls are there. They surround the entire village, cutting you off from the world, giving you a strange feeling of security and privacy but also isolation. Embedded along the ridge of the wall is a pathway, allowing you to circumnavigate the village, looking down on it from above and out across the fields and hills beyond. At one end of the praca is a walled archway, the portal into and out of the *centro storico*. It was once heavily protected, with guards in armour checking the identity and purpose of business of all who approached. Between dusk and dawn great wooden and iron gates closed across its entrance for curfew, barring any from entering or leaving the village.

Through the arch, you see the new town spread out below and I have to say, what a completely uninspiring, bland landscape of identical housing it is. We decide to walk down anyway because according to our host, the supermarket is somewhere amongst those boxes. We need to stock up for dinner tonight as well as breakfast for the next few days, as well as a little wine. It's a gradual descent into the valley of spiritless living, where colours, building styles, yards and streets are identical. Nothing stands out. Nothing appeals on any level. From down here, the view back to the *centro storico* however, is spectacular. It sits perched proudly on its high hill, insulated, self-contained, always protected by its imposing stone wall. But what really strikes you from down here, is the sea of red roofs, peaking above the walls, jutting at acute angles. Unfortunately, what you can't see from here is the spectrum of colours beneath these roofs the joyously bright blues, yellows, and whites that decorate each and every terrace. The overall impression is a vivid mixture of Greek, Swiss, Italian and Portuguese cultural colours, blended into a high spirit of appealing mélange. It's a picture that immediately lifts the spirit, brings a smile to your face. We have noticed that a number of Portuguese towns, when viewed from a distance with their houses' pervasive white walls and red roofs look almost Scandinavian. It's not until you are much closer and the other colours come into play, that the mélange unfolds. 'Obidos falls into this same pattern. The sunlight reflects off the myriad of terrace walls providing the whole village with a shining, blindingly bright façade, the beacon on the hill.

Returned from our supermarket expedition, with fresh olives, cheese, ham, eggs, chicken, spices, vegetables and several Douro wines, Wendy unpacks while I try to remember our host's instructions on using the log fire. There is a pile of wood stacked next to it, kindling and larger logs. There are specific firelighters and there is newspaper. It should be easy. Open the glass front, place all ingredients inside, light a match and *hey presto*. That's the theory. I can't for the life of me remember whether he said to start with the air vent lever up or down. Once again, I curse the inability of the middle-aged mind to retain information. I try it with the vent open. The fire lights without a problem, we're away, except.....smoke is pouring from under the glass at the front. Within minutes the room is a dark cloud of choking toxins. I shut the vent but the smoke keeps coming. I'd rather not alert Wendy. I had assured her that, "Of course I know how to operate indoor fires". Soon enough, however, she is smelling smoke and comes into the lounge, sarcastically asking how the fire is coming along. She begins coughing and races through the house opening doors and windows while casting me looks of derision. Insisting I give up any thoughts of being the least bit capable she tells me to turn the gas heater on instead.

After a night of failed endeavours but a wholesome home-cooked meal and a little too much wine, the morning stretches out before us with acres of blue sky, sun and slowly rising temperatures. Wendy wants to walk the village walls. It's the perfect day for photos so I strap my camera on and we head out to enjoy this glorious morning. There are several people already up on the wall as we climb the long, narrow stairs to its ridge. Wendy is already looking apprehensive. It doesn't bode well for a three-kilometre circuit of a high, narrow path and a surprisingly stiff breeze. I remember how much she hates heights and wonder at her choice of activity.

From the top, you can look out in any direction for mile upon mile. The land beyond is incredibly green. Fields of crops and woodland copse give way briefly to a scattering of tiny villages and lonely farm houses. The landscape flows relentlessly and without change to the horizon. You understand why the walled village was built here, with such commanding views of the land below. No enemy could hope to arrive unannounced and not completely knackered.

'Obidos is and has always been a bit of a showpiece and obviously one of the more desirable medieval destinations. Back in 1210, Dom Dinis chose 'Obidos as a wedding present for the ten-year-old king, Alfonso V and his cousin bride, who was two years his junior. Since then, fortunately, or perhaps unfortunately for the inhabitants of the town, it has been handed backwards and forwards between various Portuguese Kings, as wedding presents to their blushing brides. The inhabitants of the town also changed hands as they were invariably seen as belonging to the town and therefore the property of whichever king had gifted it. But royal fashion ensured that 'Obidos remained one of the country's most handsomely maintained and well-guarded towns.

Of course, the numerous monarchs also liked to stamp their ownership, usually in the form of a new church. The legacy today is a settlement populated with a number of these glorious religious relics, arguably the most beautiful of which is the Church of Santa Maria, although it was converted to its Christian ensemble from what had been an Arabian Mosque. And this single fact reminds the visitor that long before 'Obidos became a bargaining chip of royal bachelors courting young brides, it had been through many iterations. Today, the church stands alone and beautiful. It is by no means a large church, or particularly pretentious by Catholic church standards. But its simplicity is its appeal. There is a smallish, ornate entrance, white-washed stone walls, a moderately sized steeple, only one, and a granite courtyard. That's it. Yet thousands of tourists throng to this lonely building every year, most to look and photograph, but also to pray or just sit in quiet contemplation.

Our circumference of the town, via the wall comes to a premature end. Wendy's fear of heights has been given an unwanted shot of adrenaline by the fact that the narrow 30-inch ridge upon which we are walking, turns out to be two-way. On the first passing, Wendy flattens herself against the outside barrier and closes her eyes while two amused teenagers walk confidently around her. On the second passing, however, a rather well-fed middle-aged man beats her to the barrier, fastening himself to the wall and forcing us into the narrow space between his luxurious belly and a significant drop. At this point, Wendy descends into a mild panic, which escalates as she's forced to navigate her way around the belly. She's holding tightly onto my arm but is already white in the face and trembling. It's time to get off these walls onto the safe, open ground below.

****

It's now mid-afternoon and we're looking for somewhere suitably soothing, with no elevation whatsoever. Wendy knows just the place. We have read a bit about The Literary Man, an entire hotel dedicated to book lovers, and it's right here in 'Obidos. As it happens, the hotel is only two streets from our apartment. From the outside, it looks very upmarket, large picture-glass windows through to softly lit rooms, plenty of mahogany wood panelling, and a heavy oak door with a large silver knocker. We enter and find it just as impressive inside. There is an abundance of polished flooring, deep leather lounges, oak tables, bankers' lamps at each table and a subdued atmosphere. There are couples in leisure suits and fine silk dresses, sipping exotic looking concoctions while chatting quietly about how good they look. We don't. We have come in our walking pants, shoes and windcheaters and look very much out of place.

I order a beer and white wine while Wendy selects a table away from the best dressed of the customers. It feels like a large, extravagantly furnished library that happens to serve alcohol. Perfect really. Settling in I gaze at the walls of books that surround us, thousands of them. In fact, there are 65,000 books here, collected from all over the world and on every topic you can imagine, in numerous languages. Wendy and I select a couple each to leaf through while enjoying our second, third, then fourth beverage. It's a blissful way to pass time. Suddenly we're aware that it has become dark outside and the couples that had been gathered at tables when we entered have long gone. A new crowd is building for the dinner service and we belong even less than we did before. Time to take our slightly fuzzy heads home and cook our own dinner in time to watch the town's Easter parade tonight.

When checking in, our host had excitedly told us about this parade, encouraging us to put all aside in order to watch the procession. He told us it would be coming right past our door, proud of the fact that because of his apartment's location, we had one of the town's prime viewing spots. Tonight's procession is part of an entire Holy Week in 'Obidos which includes the Easter weekend and injects an energy into the village's churches that they otherwise rarely experience. From the village gate, the procession will pass the Church of St Mercy and St James, lead on to the Church of Santa Maria and Straight Street (an anomaly in this jungle of winding lanes), through the main village praca and then down past our apartment before doing the whole lot over again.

Like most Portuguese towns and villages, the Easter Parade has been a tradition of 'Obidos culture for longer than its residents can remember, in fact the early 17th century and, in a land where tradition is strong, there is no sign of its diminished popularity or reverence. Tonight, as the procession comes into view residents and visitors alike crowd outside their doors, hang from two-storey windows and follow in the street behind. We copy our neighbours and place lighted candles (left for this occasion) in our windows and at our front door. It is, even for the non-religious, quite a reverential experience.

The first of the parade marchers are dressed as Roman soldiers, cloaked in scarlet gowns, bronze helmets and beating a sombre, rhythmic note upon their oversized drums. There must be twenty in this first group. They range in age from about fourteen to seventy and take their roles very seriously. The onlookers are just as serious. Following, are perhaps two hundred believers, from the village, surrounding homesteads, and those who come here especially for this event. They are rugged up against the chill night air and are all carrying long, specially designed wooden rods, each with a flame dancing on its end. The followers crowd a small group of five young girls who are dressed in deep blue satin, ankle-length tunics, with large white wings attached to their small backs – the angels of the parade. This group is followed by four men in white, Arabic robes and headdress, who between them, carry a large a large white, glass enclosed crypt in which lies the mannequin of Jesus Christ. Another group with life-like mannequin of Joseph comes next, while still others carry large white crosses. The final entourage in the procession comprises ten men of all ages, wearing identical clothing with long, candle-lit poles. All are silent as they pass by, all apparently mesmerised by the significance of this events, and the ritualised messages it carries.

Whether you are a believer or not, this type of event does one thing extremely well. It forces you to think. Not about whether to believe or not believe, but about the notion that in today's world, where lives tend to be ruled by external and largely superficial forces, where we measure our time in minutes and our concentration in seconds and a Google search takes us to the next step in instant gratification, the ideas of tradition, ritual, and meaning still have a place. And that is a welcome relief.

These people have held their particular faith for two thousand years. It has become embedded in their culture, the fabric of their community, their very psyche. It is not a passing fad. It is a set of beliefs and traditions that has taken millennia to evolve and adapt. It has become deeply, profoundly ingrained in the way the community lives its daily life, what it holds important, how its members relate. This is real. You can only experience it by being part of a close-knit, family-orientated society that respects its place in history and understands a meaning of a life that perhaps some of us have tossed carelessly, foolishly aside. Add to that, the fact that these people are practising their ritual in a tiny, hilltop village that was born in the mists of time and you realise what a privilege it is to share this night.

****

It's Saturday morning. After a long walk through the village, then along a track that leads down from the eastern side through tall grasses overhung by giant beech and oak trees, we clamour up a particularly steep section to gain views across the valley. This perimeter track boasts a number of archaeological sites, where specimens from the Phoenicians, Celts and of course the Romans, have been regularly unearthed. Even more interesting, however, is the fact that on some of the lower stretches of the hill evidence of a Palaeolithic, or Old Stone Age settlement, has been detected. As yet, there are no precise dates for the finds, but the Palaeolithic era reaches from about 11,000 BC to 50,000 BC. This gives some indication of just how long people have been thinking 'Obidos is a rather nice place in which to hang out.

The foliage along this track is thick and obstructive, often blocking our way and reducing visibility to a few metres, a problem that you certainly do not encounter within the village walls. Apart from the wisteria covering many houses and walls inside the village with spectacular shades of purple and lilac, you have a hard time spotting any plants at all. This lack of flora is not unique to 'Obidos. It is something we have noticed throughout our Portuguese trip. Yes, there are abundant green fields, meadows, forests and local woodland *outside* settlements but good luck finding anything growing *within*.

It appears residents throughout this wonderful country simply like their stone, and plenty of it. Stone walls surround most historic towns, with more of them surrounding individual residences within. The houses themselves are of stone, the churches are stone and the streets and lanes are of cobbled stone. Even the 'village greens' that you come across are simply a cleared and vacant area of stone slabs that happen to have bench seats. You often share these 'greens' with parked cars or vans unloading goods. There is no hint of *green* in sight. It all gives an incredible sense of permanence, and *does* have a certain beauty, but occasionally it would be refreshing to see the odd plant.

I tried to find the reason behind this apparent aversion, why the Portuguese delight in public gardens of stunning beauty but are reluctant to transplant that same beauty to their own backyards. I came up with nothing. No internet search gives a clue and the people themselves look at you strangely when asked such a question, as if it should be obvious. Perhaps they think stone is beautiful enough. Perhaps this simple, uncrowded, unadorned domestic landscape is what gives them pleasure, the whites, fawns and greys of solid rock provide uncluttered lines that appeals to the Portuguese mind.

It's another beautiful April day but the sun is already quite intense. We can feel the back of our necks and our arms getting burnt, plus, we could really do with refreshments. Wendy suggests we head about another mile along the track to where it meets the main road coming into the village. We know that sitting at this junction is the only petrol station in town and a place where we can hopefully buy cold drinks and perhaps an ice-cream. Before too long we are approaching the lone station and surprisingly, what looks like a group of six, forty-something men and women sitting around a plastic white table with beer, glasses of wine and open crisp packets. There are several empty cans piled in the centre of the table, which suggests that this gathering has been more than a quick stop-over. These people have settled in, but on the black asphalt driveway out front. As we walk up to the station entrance we are met with friendly smiles and greetings, all in Portuguese. Perhaps this is a regular haunt of theirs. They seem happy and obviously content to relax amongst petrol fumes and bare asphalt surroundings. We buy ice-cold water bottles, ice-cream, nod our farewells and head back towards the village.

Walking back up into the *Centro Storico* we cross under a medieval stone arch, one of the village's original gates, and turn down towards a little tucked away bar we'd noticed earlier. It sits huddled within the fortified walls, is dark and cramped inside and has a very old, disused wine press in its foyer. I order us two glasses of red wine from a waiter who does all his talking with a nod of the head, and return to the tiny table Wendy has secured. The bar is silent. Couples sit and sip their wine quietly, rarely conversing. The barman moves between tables quietly collecting glasses and refilling, all with a nod, and Wendy and I are reduced to whispers for fear of upsetting the equilibrium. It's a rather austere and unsettling experience, more akin to some holy ritual than drinking.

****

Tonight, back at the apartment, I have once again failed with the indoor fire and our lounge room has taken on a grey, hazy atmosphere. Suddenly we don't feel like cooking and decide instead, on a restaurant close by that our host has recommended. It's only 6.30pm but already a line is beginning to form outside. This restaurant doesn't take bookings, so you simply turn up and hope you are early enough to secure a table. Our host had whispered in conspiratorial tones that this particular restaurant has the best chef in Óbidos. However, given the size of the village, this really didn't carry the reverence that was intended. Once inside, we're led to our cosy table in one of the restaurant's many alcoves. Soft candle-light, traditional décor and delicious scents emanating from the kitchen lift our hopes.

Several wait staff appear quickly to arrange our table and take drink orders. In a few more minutes, a young, cautious woman arrives to take our meal order. She begins rattling off the menu in Portuguese, always a sign of authenticity but not helpful to us. We apologise for our inability to understand so she rapidly turns to an abbreviated English, supported by lots of sign language and gestures. We work through each item on the menu as she attempts to explain. For what turns out to be "Beef Cheeks" she stands, as if in a game of charades, pulls her cheeks in and out rapidly. For "Pork Belly" she rubs her stomach and makes strange oinking sounds, and by the time we get to "Rump Steak" she is vigorously slapping her backside. What begins as a pantomime rapidly deteriorates into a strange song and dance routine and by now everyone is thoroughly enjoying themselves. The waitress is laughing, we're laughing and couples on each side of us have also joined the fun. Eventually, in much confusion, we complete our orders and the waitress reluctantly takes her leave. We're not quite sure what we'll end up with but it's the most fun I've had ordering a meal.

When the food arrives, it smells and looks divine. My Beef Cheeks simply fall apart in their tenderness. Wendy's Pork Belly is the best she's ever had. But like all Portuguese dishes, the meat dishes are exactly as described, with no accompaniments. Portuguese love their meat and restaurants traditionally provide generous lashings of all kinds with little or nothing else. They don't seem to really believe in vegetables or any other textures on the plate. Even for someone like me, who really appreciates a nice carnivorous meal, by this stage of the trip I'm suffering meat fatigue. Wendy, a person who is happy with vegetarian meals whenever they're on offer, is beginning to groan under the weight of this relentless onslaught.

We've discovered over the weeks that the Portuguese diet is also relatively high in fat and salt, which goes some way to explaining the general body shape. Their small Celtic frame is usually rounded out generously, even among the young. It is certainly not the healthiest of diets we've come across. Combined with the cheapness of their cigarettes and their penchant for smoking them, I can't help thinking about the issues of life expectancy and cost of health-care. Wendy and I keep reminding ourselves that as soon as we land on Australian soil, we'll be sticking to an exclusive vegetarian diet for at least a month.

On our final morning we decide to get up early and take a goodbye tour of the village, making sure we haven't missed anything. First, it's up the narrow winding alleys to the stone archway, or gate to 'Obidos. Sitting just inside the gate is a large, paved courtyard, where residents gather to chat and storekeepers set up temporary stalls in an attempt to tantalise incoming tourists. It's also a communal area in which the village hosts its local festivals and seasonal events. This morning, as with every one since we've been here, we pass a small, craven woman with short, wiry hair, a sun scorched face and too many wrinkles to count. As with every other day, she casts a tortured, weak smile as we approach and activates a small wooden contraption in her hand that imitates birdsong. She continues this as each and every person passes by, so that her old, bony hands are constantly in motion. From sun up to sun down, in the same spot, in the same clothes she persists with, as far as we can tell, very few sales. It's a dreary existence but like many in small outpost villages, where unemployment is notoriously high and welfare insufficient, people are reduced to making money any way they can. This is the other, not so glamorous reality of these historic, photogenic settlements that dot the Portuguese countryside.

What *does* surprise us as we reach the far end of the courtyard, is finding our Airbnb host setting up his unusual looking drum kit, or what is known here as a Sarronca. It's a large, flat, circular brass disk that is rubbed bare-handed by the musician in alternating rhythms to create the required notes. Our host's playing produces the most wonderful, haunting sounds, mystical and romantic at the same time. He seems an experienced musician and admits that he's been playing this instrument since childhood. But why is he busking? Surely, he doesn't need the money. He gave the impression of being pretty well off and in this village, I assume you can make quite a sum from an Airbnb. Apparently, he just loves playing, and likes to give others the same pleasure that he derives from this pastime. We stop and chat for a while, much to Wendy's pleasure and as we leave, he hands us a CD that he's recorded to take back to Australia.

After lunch, we spend our final afternoon in our private little courtyard, laid with some of the only grass in 'Obidos. Cheese, olives and Douro wine are the perfect accompaniment for our dreamy reverie on this beautiful, cool, sunny day. Sitting in recliners, facing the ancient walls above us we ponder on what brought us here, our journey together. We have experienced much so far and learned a little of this intriguing culture. We've been surprised, enchanted, had numerous myths exploded and been privileged with some unforgettable sights. But I'm hoping we have saved the best for last. From what I've read, Sintra promises to enchant in a rare and lasting way.

Sintra - The Aristocratic Neighbour

Taking the train almost directly south for just over two hours, via Lisbon, you arrive in the sought-after town of Sintra. The landscape on our journey is filled with undulating hills of woodland and fields of green. The vegetation in this area can only be described as luxurious. In between, there is a handful of small, traditional villages that weave themselves into the natural contours. The train trip is relatively uneventful, except for a glitch with a change of trains in the town of Cacém. One Portuguese timetable labels the station as Cacém. The other tells us to alight and change at Agualva- Cacém. When asking the conductor for some clarity, his response is a bored, "Is same". He points to a back page of our timetable which shows that the station, for a reason beyond my understanding, goes by either name.

Sintra station is a very different one from the ghostly relic at 'Obidos. It's busy, chaotic even, with tourists and locals scrambling in every direction. Everyone is in a hurry, scurrying past each other, hauling bags, calling out in confusion. The street leading into the station is exactly the same. It is narrow and frantic. I'm not sure if we have hit rush hour but it certainly gives that appearance. My first impressions of Sintra are disappointing considering my high expectations. Remembering that we're here for the next two weeks, I wonder if we've made some terrible mistake. This final fortnight marks the end of our stay in Portugal. It was intended to be a relaxing, wind-down phase, where we enjoy the quiet, slow-pace of a historic, regional paradise before heading home. This doesn't seem to be fulfilling that dream. Navigating our way through throngs of commuters, we eventually manage to find a taxi, provide the disinterested driver with directions to our apartment which thankfully is several miles from this mayhem.

Our taxi is out of the bustling chaos within minutes and soon we are climbing a winding, steep road with deep, untouched woodland on both sides. Our fears subside. In no more than a few minutes, we've been transported from madness to solitude. By the time we reach the gates to the historic township or the *Centro Storico*, we have climbed more than fifteen hundred feet, from the coast to the mountain. The taxi driver explains in a mixture of Portuguese, English and sign language that he can take us no further. Cars are not allowed beyond this point. Our apartment, he explains lackadaisically, is somewhere on the other side of the town square or *praca*.

Wendy and I exit the taxi and immediately hear silence. We breathe deeply of the pristine mountain air, unpolluted by car fumes or even a hint of industry. The short drive has delivered us through a portal into another time and place and it's a lot more to our liking. In fact, it is thoroughly exquisite. There are obviously two very different parts to the city of Sintra. This *centro storico*, is the realm of the time traveller. It's high, uncrowded, quiet, beautiful, highlighted by centuries-old Moorish architecture, grand manors, surrounded by lush woods and overlooked by a 12th century Moorish castle. In addition, there are not one, but two royal palaces. Nothing resembles the sterile, modern city below.

The buildings that surround the praca are tall in structure and rich in colour. Each apartment is at least two, often three stories. Many of them are now divided into several smaller apartments; others, still the individual domain of affluent owners. There are whites, salmons, deep blues, vibrant greens, yellows and many colours in between. In their midst, casting a proprietary eye over them all, is the Sintra National Palace, or Palácio da Vila, in all its regal splendour. It is vast and of dazzling white, with multiple, mustard coloured roofs. Dominating its skyline are two enormous, white cones that stretch far above the traditional roofline. These, in their day, belonged to the cavernous kitchen located in the bowels of the Palace and acted as chimneys, carrying away the smoke from a long row of substantial ovens that operated day and night.

The Palace was home to Portuguese royalty for the majority of their reign, residing here in Sintra for almost four centuries, from the mid-15th to the early 19th. They were particularly fond of the Palace because of its location in such a beautiful town, but also because of the rich agriculture to which they had easy access and the abundance of game available for hunting expeditions. Although the Palace underwent numerous early modifications and improvements, what you see today is much as it was during the Middle Ages, providing an enthralling insight into the lavish lifestyles of Portuguese Royalty and the lengths to which they went to ensure their absolute comfort at all times. Above all, though, the Palace is a thing of beauty, a monument of architectural magnificence that lends a rarefied air to the town in which it sits.

Nestled among the surrounding apartments is an array of shops, restaurants, cafes, and wine bars. And snaking away from the praca on all sides are narrow laneways, usually leading up steep hills in long, hidden meanders with tiny shops of all descriptions tucked into their edges. It's a postcard scene that tells of once great and still lingering wealth. My first impressions of historic Sintra are of an intimately preserved, richly endowed but welcoming town that promises to reveal itself, layer by layer the longer one stays and the more one explores.

Eventually, along an ancient cobblestone laneway off the north side of the praca, we find our apartment. It's behind a high, stone wall with a large iron gate, sealed off from the lane and imposing in its façade. Pressing the buzzer on the gate, we wait several minutes until we're greeted by an elegant, middle-aged woman with a cultured English accent. She is cheery and welcoming. We learn through the course of introductions that she and her husband moved from Wiltshire, UK to Sintra in 1989, buying the rather large estate that they now inhabit.

The hosts then went about building two more apartments behind their own house for the purpose of renting out, which they now do through Airbnb. We also learn in these first few minutes that she's a real professional. She's practiced in the art of hosting, knowing exactly what the customer both needs and wants. She then supplies them in abundance. It's obvious that she's been doing this for a long time and doing it well.

Their own house is substantial, beautifully adorned and sits amongst large, carefully maintained grounds. The apartment to which she leads us is, in a word, gorgeous. It is also quintessentially Sintra. Wendy gives me a look as if to say, "we've hit the jackpot here" and we both smile, knowing we will be enjoying it for the next two weeks. The interior space is large, modern but with just a hint of Moorish influence, tastefully decorated, with every convenience and comfort you could ask for.

It strikes me once again, that the neighbourhood and accommodation in which you reside while travelling, are critical to your overall impressions. For me, the monuments, castles, cathedrals or the many other points of interest that I visit in each place are not nearly as important as how that place makes me *feel*. The aesthetics of a village or town is what counts. The people who inhabit them, the contours of their history and their influence on culture, the overall *vibe*; they are what shape the way we think of a place, the way we will remember it. And, personally speaking, a significant component of that *vibe* is the place you come home to each night, the place from which you view your surroundings, the character and feel of your neighbourhood. This is part of the overall immersion. The less comfortable and at ease you are, the more difficult it is to immerse. Our Sintra apartment *feels* good. It's in tune with the rest of the *centro storico*, and allows us to feel part a part of it.

Our landlady's welcome has concluded with a cascade of walking trail ideas and the advice that we can call on her at any time for anything we might need. I look around and decide that she's not really left us in need of anything. She departs to her own house across the yard and we begin settling in for a fortnight of cultural saturation. From our front lawn are panoramic views across the valley below to the *new*, busy city of Sintra, far removed from our own solitude. If we turn and look up to the mountain behind, we can glimpse remains of the Moorish castle and the second Royal

Palace perched high on its citadel of rock and cliff-face. Both are walkable from the *centro storico*, long, steep, exhausting walks, but still walkable.

****

Roosters

Again, we are seeing roosters attached to walls and on signs around the praca. For much of our Portuguese trip, Wendy and I had been noticing a plague of roosters. These are not the feathered, crowing type, but rather, the ornamental brand. They have been everywhere, and Sintra is no exception. Plaques in front of restaurants and cafes, on flags, on coffee mugs, as fridge magnets and on tea towels. Bright in colour, mixing blues, yellows, reds and blacks, they are often hand painted and present as a cheery, rather proud emblem. Although they increasingly mystified us, for a reason that I am yet to justify, we had never attempted to understand their significance. But finally, that time has come.

Legend has it that the Rooster of Barcelos rose to prominence in the 17th century for its heroic defence of an innocent man sentenced to death. To lend the story some moral weight, the tale hinges on the fact that the poor fellow had been passing through the city of Barcelos on a pilgrimage when a wealthy and unjust landowner (as they always seem to be) accused him of stealing his silver. When taken to the local magistrate's house in the midst of his sumptuous dinner party, the innocent man pointed at the roasted rooster on the dining table and cried that as surely as he was innocent, this rooster would crow at his hanging.

Sure enough, as the noose was slipped around the prisoner's neck later that night, the deceased, overcooked rooster stood up from the table and let forth a deafening crow. The magistrate left his guests and rushed to the scene of the hanging, demanding that the prisoner be released. The moral of the story is, of course, *that the poor and defenceless, particularly those of a religious bent, are always persecuted by the rich and powerful, but somehow, their virtue will save them in the end*. Nevertheless, the Portuguese have taken to this particular legend with gusto and with the fervent encouragement of the Catholic Church. Now, whenever we see this little symbol, we have a quiet chuckle and understand, with new appreciation, the entrenched beliefs of this people.

Speaking of symbols, another captivating if somewhat peculiar attraction located on the edge of town contains overt Templar symbols, harking back to our experiences in Tomar. These are housed within the estate of the Quinta da Regaleira, a tourist hotspot. Crowds stream along the roadway, line up at the main gate and pay a not too inconsequential sum to enter the magnificent grounds. It's a warm day and progress is slow, as large gatherings mill noisily around each of the attractions and congest pathways between intricately laid out gardens. The gardens themselves host a palace of their own, as well as a small chapel, a lake, grottos, exotic plants and a myriad of tunnels, fountains and other follies.

After being sold on by the Baroness of Regaleira in 1892, the new owner, one Antonio Carvalho Monteiro, an entomologist and eccentric millionaire, went about transforming the estate's ten acres into a type of Victorian Disneyland. In his spare time he continued to build on his inherited fortune by selling coffee to Brazil, providing a stream of funds to continue his extraordinarily aberrant work. Perhaps Antonio's most bizarre creation is located at a lower corner of the grounds, surrounded by artificial garden pools filling from hidden caves and full of giant lilies. Buried within this patch of soil is a spiral, layered, stone tunnel that descends directly underground for some twenty-seven metres. This, he labelled the “initiation tunnel”. His idea was that one must begin at the bottom, and work his way up through the spiral staircase, in the process, experience a rebirthing of the soul. Wendy insists that we undergo this transformation and along with a myriad of others we tramp our way up this dizzying enclosure. But the only change I notice when emerging at the top is a shortness of breath and fuzzy head. What a strange and uncertain imagination this fellow had.

****

Morning ritual

The breakfast surprise on Tuesday morning is outside our door on white plates. Two large grapefruit cut into quarters await us, with a note from the host that they were picked from her organic tree in the courtyard. After such a thoughtful gesture the least we could do is to make quick work of them with our toast and coffee. What a treat they are. Delicious, sweet with a tang, and full of juice. There is nothing quite like home grown fruit. We are also soon to discover that these grapefruit would be a morning ritual and the beginning of an easy friendship with the owner. As the barriers of formal reserve are relaxed in favour of the owner's natural friendliness and warmth, the grapefruit are delivered in person, with a smile and usually a ten-minute chat about our plans for the day. The host is also a committed walker and provides us with plenty of routes for the best views and least used tracks.

Our plan this morning is to make the trek up to the Moorish Castelo, or Castle. First, we make our way across the praca to gain bearings and more importantly, find the tourist office. Wendy is keen to purchase a map of the area. Wendy is *always* keen to purchase maps of areas. We find the office, ask about the best track to the Castelo, and Wendy immerses herself in the map section. I take no interest in this, as I find it impossible to read maps of any description. With Wendy, it's an obsession. Her excitement levels rise dramatically whenever she comes across a place that may happen to sell maps, and once purchased, it's like a new toy. Not that her map-reading skills have been elevated through this interest. Sometimes we find the right track, often we don't. Even when finding said track, we usually fail to stay on it. But this doesn't seem to dent her enthusiasm.

After purchasing a large, detailed, multi-fold map we head back out to the praca to be confronted by a blast of heavy rock music that shatters the morning quiet. It's erupting from a tiny bar on the other side of the square, nestled between traditional cafes. Bewilderingly, several customers are sitting drinking coffee, attempting to communicate over the noise. The music is none other than the work of Australian rock group ACDC. Now I have to admit that as an Australian who grew up listening to this band, a wave of nostalgia and even a smidgen of patriotism sweeps over me. For a moment I'm lost in a youthful reverie. I am also reminded of ACDC's global appeal but then learn that this particular bar is owned and operated by an Australian, who's been living here for the past ten years and wants everyone else to love this band as much as he does. And, while a little nostalgia is a good thing, I can't help but think that this music, at this volume, in the quiet *centro storico*, is more than a little incongruous. Depending on how you're feeling at the time, such a barrage of decibels may be annoyingly unpleasant or, in fact, may simply be part of the contrasting aesthetics that makes small town Portugal so appealing.

For now, however, we steer clear of these violent soundwaves, instead, trying to decipher the origins of the Castelo track somewhere ahead. Eventually, we find the track off a narrow, heavily wooded road leading out of the historic centre and along which we're told Madonna owns one of Portugal's largest mansions. Deciding on a whim to delay our walk for thirty minutes or so, Wendy suggests we skip further along the road to cast our eye upon this splendour of celebrity extravagance. The road is bordered on each side by deep, lush woodland that blankets sound and guarantees seclusion. By now, we're the only two on this road and feel as if we may be somehow trespassing even though the residence is still unseen. The surrounding birdlife has also fallen silent, as if fearful of what our provocative wanderings may induce.

It's not too long before the road narrows even further and replacing the woods is a towering, seemingly impenetrable wall of stone that extends into the far distance. On and on the wall continues, barring any hope of a view, casting gloom over the road ahead, leading us relentlessly on. After another 250 metres or so, a substantial, black metal gate with "Private" and "Keep Out" blazed across its thick bars rears up in front.

Already this place is shouting 'exclusive' but in a very *public* way. Behind the gate and beyond a long, dramatic driveway, stands a great stone mansion that few in Portugal would rival. There are arches to break the monotony of its unimaginative size and medieval turrets ring the upper section, which smacks ever so slightly of Hollywood. You may be forgiven for calling it a palace rather than a mansion (or a villa as I'm later to learn). It's of what they call Moorish revival architecture, is rumoured to be more than 16,000 square feet in size, has four bedrooms but seven bathrooms, a fifteen-car garage, as well as sporting a two-bedroom caretaker cottage. It all sits within a meticulously manicured garden setting that is large enough to accommodate a new housing estate.

The mansion was apparently purchased to provide the ageing pop star with a secluded, private residence to which she could escape and avoid the constant limelight and celebrity. The secluded façade evaporated quickly, however. In a very short time the singer had put herself on the wrong side of the gentle Sintra folk by establishing no-parking zones far and wide around the property and filming her music videos at the residence, with all the attendant film, sound and make-up crews coming and going in what the locals claimed was a manner at odds with their peaceful paradise.

I wonder if the celebrities who claim to crave privacy and solitude, actually *do*. Or perhaps their idea of privacy is just very different to mine. Because, even when they 'try' to get away from it all, they manage, somehow, to bring it all with them. Perhaps they become so caught up in the celebrity atmosphere that to lock themselves away in absolute solitude is much the same as an alcoholic going 'cold turkey'. It's too much of a shock. Too removed. Maybe solitude and privacy are only desirable when on public display, when you can be *seen* to seek seclusion. After all, if no one knows you're there, what's the point? Maybe I'm just too cynical, maybe not.

Costelo dos Mouros

We leave the mansion and publicity behind, turn back to our own road. The uphill trek to Sintra's Castelo awaits. The Costelo dos Mouros, or Castle of the Moors, was built through the 8th and 9th centuries, remaining a Moorish stronghold until being captured by the Christians during the mid-12th century. It then underwent further fortification during the mid and late 14th century, even though its strategic significance by this time was waning. Territorial manoeuvring and conquest had moved on to other parts of Portugal, leaving Lisbon and Sintra, at least for the moment, in relative peace. By the early 15th century, the Castle had become neglected by the great powers, its chapel instead becoming home to a small Jewish community, which occupied it for the next fifty years. This gathering was eventually persecuted and expelled, like their equally persecuted cousins around the globe.

Today, the Castelo stands as a fractured reminder of how our medieval ancestors used to live and protect themselves. Although crumbling in many places and without its numerous walls and internal structures, it remains regal. It still watches proudly over the *centro storico* below, and for the next two weeks we'll witness it casting long shadows in the early morning light, or taking on an ethereal beauty as a setting sun turns its walls and crumbling turrets into deep hues of crimson and mauve. As night falls, its great dark mass will lend a sombre, warning tone from the hillside above.

No sooner do we set foot on the track than Wendy decides a toilet break is required. Well, there's none on this track so it's back to the tourist bureau in the praca. Sometime later we try again. A family we had met in Coimbra several weeks ago warned us about the inclines in Sintra and after a mere fifteen minutes on this track, I realise that they weren't exaggerating. It's steep. Really steep. And relentless. Each time you think there may be a plateau in sight, the illusion evaporates and subjects you to more climbing. An hour in, with numerous stops to catch our breath and still we're climbing. Curses and disgruntled mumbles in a range of accents and languages surround us as other walkers think the same way, heaving their tired bodies slowly up this tortuous incline. Soon, the Castelo is in plain sight ahead, but its proximity is a mirage. For all our climbing it doesn't seem any closer. Several older tourists are already turning back and grudgingly wishing us luck as they pass. One couple just smiles weakly and plod on down.

An hour passed and many more walkers appear to be coming down the track than going up. I wonder if they have already visited the castle or just given up somewhere ahead and simply turned around. Passers-by greet us either in a stilted Portuguese or more usually, their own unique language. There is a constant stream of multinational languages being thrown our way and my middle-aged brain is having difficulty coping. First, I am trying to work out what they're saying and then, attempting to form a reply either in my own special version of Portuguese or a sawn-off English variation. By the time I have come up with something acceptable, they've usually passed. Finally, it becomes all too much. When one unsuspecting tourist gives me the traditionally shortened Spanish greeting of Ullo, my neural fuses spasm. I blurt out a strangled "Mama". He immediately casts a bewildered, then wary eye on me before passing as quickly as possible. Wendy, who has heard my greeting gives me an incredulous look and asks, "What was that?"

"I really don't know," I reply, at which she bursts out laughing, but for the remainder of the walk, drops little comments about the debilitating effects of senility. I also begin thinking on this subject more than is comfortable.

Finally, we're almost upon the Castelo. Turning around, the views across the valley to Sintra's *centro storico* are stunning. Vast, sweeping, tree-filled valleys open up into a broad vista in which sits the praca, its two and three-story apartments encircling the open space, the grand Palace dominating the entire scene and then another sweep down through valleys to the new town with its endless bustle. From here, the *centro storico* looks a work of art. Bright, colourful, reds and whites arranged in a neat semi-circle across the valley floor. The town boasts sensual curves and delicate architecture, blending naturally into the hillside. A symphony of man-made and natural panoramas that bewitch the senses. It is now, from this vantage point, at this time, that I really fall in love with Sintra. I want to go on throwing adjectives at it, but it's hard to translate, to convey the way these colours and curves nestle among trees and shallow, broad clefts create their own aesthetic wonderland.

With others who have made it this far, Wendy and I trek the walls of the Castelo. This 1100 year old relic fascinates. You wonder what life was like here, of the battles fought, lost and won, the fear of a strange and hostile world awaiting on the other side. I cannot help but think of these castles in winter a thousand years ago, for they are barren, cold, remote, unwelcoming places. The cold would seep into the walls and remain locked there for an eternity. There would be little, if any comfort. No central heating, no lounges, no comfortable beds, just hard, granite walls that have no sympathy for the weary knight or the starving community within. And up here, on this wind-swept mountain, where temperatures dive far lower than at lesser altitudes, a place where snows come and stay, isolating you for months in your stone grave. I give an involuntary shiver.

Our return trip down the mountain takes us through the Villa Sassetti, on a footpath linking Sintra's historical centre with the Moorish Castle above. The property was built by Victor Carlos Sassetti in the late 1800s on a 1200sqm strip of land that stretches either side of the footpath. It was designed to blend what the owner interpreted as the cultural and natural landscapes of the surrounding town. The house, keeper's cottage and various outbuildings lie between twisting paths and established waterways, creating a poetically pleasurable landscape for all who travel to the relic beyond. It's a gorgeous finale to our walk.

We realise on our return to the apartment that while we have a bottle of wine to accompany dinner, we don't *actually* have any dinner. We're tired and hungry but decide that our waistlines can't handle another restaurant so soon. Instead, we opt for the Pingo Doce supermarket in the new town to stock up for several days and save some return trips. It's a good thirty-five minute walk each way, which includes many steps, steep valleys and narrow, treacherous shoulders along busy roads. Dragging our weary bones back out of our warm, comfortable apartment we face another hour or so of walking, half of it with heavy backpacks. The day has been too long. I keep thinking of the food and wine that we can indulge in on our return. At that moment, I decide that another bottle of red will be required. Wendy, at first replies with her almost mandatory, "No we shouldn't," but soon, as usual, agrees.

At the top of the stairs down into the first valley, we come face to face with a middle-aged, somewhat heavily set American couple. They are puffing and panting and the fellow is holding his side with a pained expression. The woman triumphantly exclaims, between laboured breaths, that they have just climbed "all these stairs". I'm not sure how to reply to this but Wendy, as diplomatic as ever, pipes up in congratulatory tones, agreeing that they're long and steep. The woman smiles broadly in grateful acknowledgement while her partner continues in pained silence.

"Where have you been today?" she asks. Wendy explains that we have spent most of the day at the Castle and unfortunately, we now have to head down for food. The woman squints up at the Castle high in the mountain and asks how we got there. When we admit that we walked, her smile vanishes and her bottom jaw drops. Wendy quickly chimes in that we are, however, exhausted, that it was longer than we thought and that we'll certainly sleep well tonight. Our new friend isn't mollified. Her husband simply looks at us as if we might be a bit touched. They struggle on past without further comment. After combatting more hills, steps, narrow tracks and wayward shopping bags, I'm inclined to think we *are* a bit touched, and more than ready for those two bottles of wine.

Romance

Tonight, after dinner we take a stroll into the praca to mingle with other strollers. There must be forty or fifty people here, mostly couples wandering in the still, mild evening. Quiet has descended on the *centro storico*. The bars are subdued, soft music filters from doorways. Couples sit, talking in muted tones, others window shop. A gentle breeze stirs the Palace's flags. All is watched over by the Castelo above; that great stone relic, which today was the centre of attention, with people milling across its walls and photographing its every crevice. Tonight, it sits proudly in quiet solitude, a sombre, brooding mood, its lights providing an eerie portrait of a time long past. And down here, in this large, central praca, amongst the graceful architecture of bordering apartments and the mighty Palace dominating all, you feel a sense of belonging, a feeling that here, now, all is right with the world. We sit, listening to the ancient rhythm of this special, alluring place.

The next evening, our host arrives for another chat, with the excuse that she has come to restock the fridge. Each day she arrives with another item that we may or may not need. Tonight, she seems keen to tell us some of her history, about her arrival in Portugal and the reasons for her decision. Emotions are revealed and life stories relished. She has lived in Portugal for the past twenty-nine years and in her words, "is still getting used to it". But she is happy here. She and her husband have created a fulfilling life running a successful Airbnb, and establishing themselves as 'locals'. Friends and family visit regularly from her home country, treating the trip as an exotic vacation, particularly the grandchildren. She also repays the visits, when her Airbnb bookings allow. Her energy and enthusiasm are contagious and it is obvious she loves interacting with guests.

****

Dining out in Portugal is unusually frustrating for a coeliac. Tonight is no different. Trying a restaurant only 300 metres from our apartment, a restaurant with an old stone façade, small, homely and almost full inside, we figure it should be a good bet. The strong, spicy scents emanating from its narrow doorway seem to confirm our thinking. We reason that because Sintra is more affluent than the average Portuguese city, is visited by cosmopolitan and experienced foodies from Lisbon, it should have a greater understanding of different food requirements. But such thinking would be rash.

I ask the first waiter who approaches if they have many gluten free dishes. He looks at me with a slightly bewildered look and shrugs his shoulders. Wendy rolls her eyes at me and curtly says that I need to provide the Portuguese version for the fellow. She pipes up with a big smile and says, “Livre de gluten?” But gets exactly the same response. Wendy and I look at each other while the waiter trots hurriedly back to the kitchen. A moment later a young, efficient looking waitress emerges with the fellow in tow. She looks at me questioningly and I repeat the request. “We have some,” she states. She proceeds by showing me all the dishes I *can’t* eat on the menu, but I notice they contain cheese. I tell her that I can, in fact, eat cheese, as I'm not allergic to dairy, just gluten. She looks at me in a confused way, shrugs and says, "I'm not sure." I smile weakly, thank her and explain that we can't risk it. We leave and head back down to our now familiar Pingo Doce supermarket.

After a late, hurriedly thrown together dinner, washed down with slightly more wine than was good for us, we awake sluggishly the next day. It's decided that we'll take things easy for the morning and rest our sore heads. That is until there's a sharp rap on the door. It's our friendly, all too energetic host. She's arrived with her morning gift of two enormous grapefruit, cut lovingly into little cubes. Wendy thanks her and asks if she'd like a coffee. She accepts enthusiastically and plonks herself down at the kitchen table, already chatting happily and asking what we have planned for today. Sheepishly I suggest that we thought we might have a lazy morning.

"Rubbish," she says. "It's a beautiful, sunny day. You need to get out and enjoy it. I think you should do the walk up to the Pena Palace. That'll let you know you're alive."

"We don't feel too alive at the moment," Wendy responds.

"Oh nonsense. It'll do you the world of good" and with that, she grabs our map and marks out the best route, which includes a dreaded *short-cut* along part of the road before heading into deep woods and cutting across above the Castelo. "This will knock a good half hour off your walk," she states.

After a quick coffee (she does everything quickly) she's up and telling us she wants to hear all about it this afternoon. With that, she's gone, as quickly and efficiently as she came.

Wendy and I drag ourselves into showers, have another coffee in hopes of inspiration, lace up walking shoes and head out the door. You can see the Pena Palace from almost anywhere in the *centro storico* with its brightly coloured towers, turrets and walls. It mixes hues of startling yellows with reds, blacks, greys and oranges in a most *unregal* way. From here, it looks impossibly far away, perched atop the highest cliff in Sintra, piercing clouds swirling around its cone and with no obvious path of approach. Initially, we follow the signs and this seems to be working out nicely. But Wendy is keen to try the host's suggested shortcut. I remind her of our disastrous track record with shortcuts and point out that this won't be improved by lingering hangovers. Instead, I suggest we just stay on this path with everyone else. She responds with something about my middle-aged lack of adventure, followed by a mischievous smile that I always give in to. It looks like we're taking the shortcut.

The first fifteen minutes of the journey are punctuated by Wendy's lengthy snippets on the Palace history. She tells me it is one of Portugal's greatest symbols of Romantic architecture, a rambling five-storey, thirteen-bedroom, twelve-bathroom mansion. Its earliest iterations can be traced back to the late 15th century when the then king, Manuel I, fell in love with the mountain above his playground of Sintra. Deciding he wanted God close at hand for easy confessions, he ordered a monastery to be built on its highest peak.

A later rebuild in the mid-1800s was to a much more refined standard than earlier attempts, being overseen by King Ferdinand 11. Like most kings of the time, and probably still many today, Ferdinand had a mistress. *Unlike* many mistresses, however, this one had an unusual hold over him, placing herself in a position to demand, rather than request. She insisted on living in close proximity to the King and to be fair, he wanted her close by. His love for her was a talking point among Sintra's local aristocracy. He built her a small castelo of her own at the bottom of his garden, far enough away and out of sight of his increasingly jealous wife, but close enough for nightly visits. She was content for only a little time with this arrangement and provided the King with an ultimatum; if he wished to retain her services, which he most certainly did, then he must also secure her a large Swiss chalet, in which she could holiday when the mood took her. Unsurprisingly, she received it. His love for her continued to grow in inverse proportion to that for his wife and when the wife finally died, he brought his mistress up the hill to the main Palace and made her his new wife. Her mission was complete but the demands never ceased.

Apparently, the Palace's latest design was inspired by the Templar monastery in Tomar, although one may be forgiven for attributing its fantastical appearance to Walt Disney. To me, it looks more like a Disneyworld medieval theme park, being doused with such flamboyant splashes of gaudy colour that you really have to wonder at King Luis' state of mind. It is completely incongruous with the surrounding landscape and architecture of Sintra, a plaything of a king with far too much imagination and no one game enough to rein it in. However, he did die the year the Palace was completed and you can only conclude that perhaps it was of shame. Today, as part of the area of Sintra, it is listed under UNESCO World Heritage and serves as one of Portugal's most popular tourist sites.

We have yet to see the inside of the Palace as our 'shortcut' is beginning to show ominous reminders. The trail has led to the narrow winding road which snakes its way from the *centro storico* all the way up to the front entrance of the Palace, about five hundred metres from the actual building. Our host advised that we should keep to the road for two or three hundred metres until we see a clear track leading off to the left. This will take us onto another, little used track directly to the Palace. I'm guessing that we've now been following the road for far more than the two or three hundred metres and believe me, it's not pleasant. You see, most of the tourists who travel to the Palace don't like the idea of walking. Some enterprising local residents, usually young men with just enough money to buy a tiny, three-wheel Tuk Tuk, have taken full advantage of this laziness. For a sum of €10 they will ferry you from the *centro storico* to the Palace entrance with a well-practiced, monotone summary of its history thrown in.

This is all well and good except that there are literally hundreds of these obnoxious little Tuk Tuks running on two-stroke, lawn-mower engines, making an almighty racket, and belching clouds of choking blue smoke all the way. Sharing the roadway with them is a nightmare; one which our host failed to mention. In some areas of Portugal, they have introduced low emission or even electric Tuk Tuks to help combat air pollution but not here in Sintra. Our tempers getting shorter by the step, we battle for road space with the toxic contraptions as they attempt to pass one another in a race to deliver, by now, unappreciative passengers. In fact, as Wendy and I round one corner, a Tuk Tuk is pulling off to the side of the road while a distressed female passenger staggers out onto the road and empties her stomach of that morning's breakfast.

The surrounding chaos has diverted our attention from correct pathways and we seem condemned to a road that will add hours to the walk. A family emerging from thick woods to the right of the road look even worse off than us. The mother and daughter are in the middle of a raging argument, the father is sweating profusely and the little boy looks like he's given up. The father approaches and asks almost desperately if we know where the track to the

Palace might be located. "We've been trying to find it for the past hour", he complains.

"Sorry, but we're in the same situation," I reply. We shrug shoulders, Wendy and I continuing on, leaving the family looking suicidal. But just as our own stamina and tempers are reaching flashpoint, a fit, colourfully leotarded fellow on a mountain bike comes bouncing onto the road from a track to our left. My excitement gets the better of me and I jump out in front of his bike, almost upending both of us. With some considerable annoyance he shudders to a stop and frowns. I ask where he just came from while Wendy apologises for my behaviour. "Yes," he tells us, he has just ridden down from the Palace.

"On that track?" I ask.

Grasping the fact that I'm a little slow, he responds, "Of course" and rides off.

The despondent family of four suddenly materialises beside us and with moods lifted, the six of us are on our way. The track is uphill and winding but far more pleasant than the road. Before another hour has passed, we're approaching the entrance gates where the dozens of Tuk Tuks drivers, having delivered agitated passengers, are collecting fees. There is one shop at the gate selling tickets and another selling refreshments. They're both doing a roaring trade.

A look beyond the gate shows just how magnificent the Palace grounds are. Acres and acres of manicured gardens with sweeping lawns, grandiose fountains, ponds with miniature castles in their centre, exotic palms, tiny, perfect woodlands and meandering pathways create an oasis of calm and beauty. In total, there are just under five hundred acres of this exquisite tranquillity, the entirety having been designed by King Fernando II. The man was something of a plant lover, obtaining weird and wonderful species from all over the world to fill his garden. He often strolled along these paths, appreciating and rearranging his plants to fit with his latest fantasy. But they are a credit to his vision and perseverance and in my humble opinion, eclipse the spectacle of his Palace above. In fact, Wendy and I delay our tour of the residence for as long as possible just to gain more time in which to walk amongst this wonderfully crafted and cared for landscape.

At last, reaching the Palace, we're greeted with a monotonously long queue of weary tourists waiting for their turn on the domestic merry-go-round. Security officers are allowing groups of thirty or so at a time to enter and patience among the crowd is wearing thin. The only form of entertainment during this long wait is an elderly Japanese woman feverishly taking *selfies*. She is darting backwards and forwards to stand in front of turrets, the gate, a watch-tower, and even snapping herself standing in the queue. It's a marvellous lesson in self-awareness, or *lack* of it. People are nodding towards her and giggling as she lines herself up for another artistic portrait, but she's oblivious. The love affair between her and her camera is all consuming; the people around her mere background props for the frame in which she stars.

When we finally *do* manage to squeeze into the doorway with a press of other despairing visitors, the proportions within shock. The interior is tiny, almost as if we have stepped into a shrunken model of the real thing. Rooms, receptions halls, corridors, are all in miniature. It's as if the King spent so much money on the actual building and grounds that he simply ran out of funds when it came to the interior. Making it even more claustrophobic is the number of people squeezed in here. We are shoulder to shoulder, stomach to rump, inching our way from one disappointing room to the next. After an hour of playing sardines Wendy gives me a look to say she's had enough. So have I. We slip out a side door, leaving our fellow sufferers behind and begin the descent to the bottom, the bottle shop, our apartment and a large glass of vino.

In a third of the time it took to climb to the top, we're back in the *centro storico* and into our favourite bottle shop. The owner knows us well by now, as this has become a daily visit. There is a welcome smile and an announcement that some new wine has arrived that we might like to try. Why not? Loaded up with essential supplies, it's back to our apartment for the usual ritual. Out come olives, cheese, crackers, some fresh fruit, which our ever-thoughtful host has left, and two oversized wine glasses. Music is switched on and we begin preparing tonight's dinner. It sounds simple enough, perhaps boring to some but Wendy and I love this time. We're alone, away from people and noise, cooking our favourite local produce, while chatting about the day, planning for tomorrow and lubricating the whole routine with what we hope will be some of Portugal's nicer wine.

A jewel in the crown

A new day dawns. After castigating ourselves for that second bottle of wine we gather our wits and decide a cleansing walk in the Sintra hills will work wonders. Our host has provided a list of potential walks that will take us up, away from the town and the tourist routes and thankfully, it includes no shortcuts. The track we're walking today is about eight kilometres, or five miles and will take us through forests of eucalypts (a reminder of home) as well as huge acacias and pines. The forest track is narrow at times, at others opening on to splendid vistas where you can see the coastline far below bordering the great Atlantic Ocean. Although it's even cooler up here, the ascent is steep and sweat flows freely. It's quite a workout, but one of the most enjoyable I can imagine. You are confronted constantly by dramatic views and vast, majestic residences perched in the most splendid positions, taking advantage of their surroundings. The oldest residence up here actually dates back to the 12th century, now a hostel. Still very much of the style in which it was built, the Almaa, as it's called, is laced with long, dark corridors, small rooms, smaller windows and an eeriness that never quite leaves. But it was elegant in its time, as evidenced by the nine acres of beautiful grounds that still separate it from the other residences.

I'm never exactly sure what particular label these residences fall under. You see, in Australia we have units (small), villas (not quite as small), houses (larger) and mansions (largest). But in places like Portugal and Italy the terminology is very different. Most of the residences up here in the hills are called "villas", and they are actually very large, often palatial structures, usually on an acreage and owned by the wealthy elite. In no way do they resemble our villas back home. But then there are also Quintas that to me, look much the same as the villas. Apparently, the distinction is land. You can call your villa a Quinta if it sits astride rich, arable land that in the past would have been worked by peasants. The title of Quinta is largely an aristocratic hangover from a time when the occupants didn't have to do any of the work themselves. In addition, there are several Castelos, putting their occupants one more step up the social ladder. They still don't do any of the work themselves.

Perhaps that's why this particular mountain is referred to as the "Sacred Mountain". The religious would argue it's sacred because of its holiness, its closeness to God. I would suggest it is instead consecrated by money. Up here, in the serenity of the hills, away from the buzz and distraction below, these grand estates have always and continue to provide the very rich with their own form of paradise and that is all the consecration they need.

That's the way it has been for the past three hundred years, a playground of the aristocracy and others with great wealth but no title. A mark of their cultural sophistication and the depth of their pockets was to own summer estates here in the Sintra Hills, where they would subtly compete with neighbours by filling their rooms with exotic collections from the rest of Europe. They would entertain with lavish parties, inviting celebrities, famous poets, artists and writers, composers and later, film stars to be conspicuously on 'show' for the town to witness. Hans Christian Anderson, Lord Byron (who spent much of his life in exotic seaside resorts) Strauss and William Burnett were just the a few of the many invited artists and writers to entertain and dazzle in this town. This was the age of Romanticism and Sintra was very much at the epicentre.

Even today, Sintra's nature parks, exotic gardens, Michelin restaurants and stunning views continue to seduce residents and visitors alike. So much so that international conferences, as well as economic retreats commonly choose Sintra as an 'essential' destination. They come, they stay and they play, often as guests in various villas or Quintas and from this visual sanctuary, determine the way the rest of us should be governed. The town has hosted G7 meetings, World Bank conferences, and even the notoriously secretive Bilderberg conference, in which the world's most powerful politicians and selected billionaires plan economic and political directions for the next decade. Importantly, Sintra also has the reputation as being the place in which the famous Lisbon Treaty was signed, a treaty that was to become the foundation for the European Union. But against this celebrity backdrop, the town's cultural and historic landscape remains very much an essential destination for those simply wanting to taste unrivalled beauty and the intrigue of human civilisation.

Returning from our walk we realise that we must, yet again, make the laborious trip down to the supermarket for tomorrow's breakfast supplies. When we complain to our host about the hundreds of stairs and steep hills that must be endured each time, she looks at us curiously and asks which way we walk. Wendy outlines the route we take, *turning left at the Palace, heading down the first set of many stairs, through the valley, up the steep adjoining hill, past the police station, through the gardens, along the heavily trafficked road, across the railway lines and finally, the supermarket.* As Wendy is describing this route our host is already giggling.

"Why do you take that route?" she asks. "It's probably the longest possible route there is."

Wendy and I share a look of dismay. "We thought that is the *only* route."

"Oh God no. Let me show you," and out comes one of the maps she has left us and she outlines a direct and very short route right to the supermarket.

That afternoon we take the map with us and follow her route religiously. And in about a quarter of the time it normally takes we're at the supermarket's front door. We haven't encountered any steps, any valleys, any hills, just a slow, easy descent along a quiet, tree-lined, backroad. It's only taken ten tortuous days before the obvious route is revealed.

For our last night Wendy has decided we're not cooking and opts for another of the host's restaurant recommendations. This is one of the few we have come across where they actually know what "gluten free" means and even have GF options on their menu. Already, I'm sold. As we order, two young women, looking a little tired and bedraggled sit down at the table next to us. Soon we hear American accents and talk of time on the "trail". As strangers often do, we strike up a conversation.

They have spent a month walking the El Camino de Santiago trail, a vast network of tracks that famously took pilgrims on their journey from all over Europe to their final destination of the shrine of St James, in northwest Spain. Much of the track runs through both France and Portugal and thousands of modern-day pilgrims, tourists, walkers and adventurers take to it annually. Most don't walk its entire length but rather, opt for certain sections according to preference. We had seen markers for the trail in both Lisbon and Porto but most people take up the trail in Spain, often causing considerable congestion in the height of summer. The pilgrimage was at the height of its religious popularity in the late Middle Ages but over the last two decades it has witnessed a resurgence, though perhaps not primarily of religious purpose.

These two young women are weary and in need of rest and relaxation, away from what they remembered as bad Spanish food, high prices and far too many people. Apart from these drawbacks, their time on the trail was what they describe as life-altering, an experience that has left them changed people. We share stories of our time in Portugal, which they devour with real enthusiasm as they're now spending another three weeks touring this Spanish neighbour. But silence reigns supreme as our meals are delivered and hunger takes over.

For our last night in Sintra and indeed, Portugal, it is a fitting end. Like passing a baton, we share our experiences with two fellow travellers, eager to enjoy this unique country as much as we have. Finally, we say our farewells, wish them luck and take a final stroll around Sintra's historic praca. We return to the apartment in a fulfilled but melancholy mood. Both of us have loved Sintra so much, the rarefied spirit of a mountain-top haven. What a journey this has been. Each of the destinations we have chosen – Porto, the Douro Valley, Coimbra, Tomar, Lisbon, Obidos and finally, Sintra – has been so rewarding in its own way; each offering intriguing insights into aspects of Portuguese life, culture and history. Each with its own special story to tell and its own way of telling it.

Portugal is an endearing country, filled with charm. It's a country that has seamlessly blended thousands of years of disparate histories, ethnologies and races. And the result is a powerful narrative of inspired multiculturalism, in which each heritage has its own expression and recognised identity, perhaps one of the most harmonious narratives I have encountered. It's a story that has been woven through the very fabric of the country, complementing physical beauty and breathtaking history with an inimitable human voice. You cannot help but love Portugal. You delight in memories of a heart-warming encounter, a city praca filled with life, a night of music, a walk among vineyards or the simple flow of a river.

But for me, and I think for Wendy too, Sintra represents the pinnacle of our Portuguese experience. Its tranquil, enduring rhythm is the perfect way to end our trip, the culmination of all that is so beguiling about this narrow strip of a peninsula that precipitated much of Western civilisation. Of course, I will return to Portugal, but I wish never to leave Sintra.

Made in United States
Orlando, FL
29 November 2024

54640101R00157